APPLYING
SUN TZU's ART OF WAR IN
CORPORATE
POLITICS

KHOO KHENG-HOR

APPLYING SUN TZU's ART OF WAR IN CORPORATE POLITICS

Spiced with real-life illustrations and observations, it is written in a breezy style that allows for easy reading, understanding and retention.

Pelanduk Publications

Published by
Pelanduk Publications (M) Sdn. Bhd.,
24 Jalan 20/16A, 46300 Petaling Jaya,
Selangor Darul Ehsan, Malaysia.

Address all correspondence to
Pelanduk Publications (M) Sdn. Bhd.,
P.O. Box 8265, 46785 Kelana Jaya,
Selangor Darul Ehsan, Malaysia.

Perpustakaan Negara Malaysia   Cataloguing-in-Publication Data

Khoo, Kheng-Hor, 1956- .
    Applying Sun Tzu's art of war in corporate politics / Khoo
    Kheng-Hor.
    ISBN 967-978-543-2
    1. Office politics. 2. Corporate culture. 3. Organizational behavior.
    I. Title.
    658.4095

Printed in Malaysia by
Academe Art & Printing Services Sdn. Bhd.

This book is dedicated to those
who use their power wisely.

CONTENTS

CONTENTS

THE AUTHOR

AS a business executive, consultant, author and speaker, Khoo Kheng-Hor has been described as a contemporary interpreter of Sun Tzu's treatise, *Art of War*. He has been interviewed on television and newspapers for his creative interpretations of Sun Tzu's war principles for use, not only in strategic management but also in specific areas of management such as marketing, customer service and human resource management, and now corporate politics.

Besides being the Managing Director of Stirling Training & Management Consultants Pte. Ltd., his own firm which assists clients in planning and implementing strategies and motivating their executives through his specially-developed "Management: the Sun Tzu Way" program, he is also Country Manager and Director of Adia Personnel Services Pte. Ltd. in Singapore, a member of the Swiss-based Adia International which operates over 1,900 offices worldwide to provide innovative and creative staffing solutions for clients.

His other books include *War at Work: Applying Sun Tzu's Art of War in Today's Business World*, *Sun Tzu's Art of War*, *Personnel Management Manual*, *Sun Tzu and Management* and *Personnel Policies*.

ACKNOWLEDGEMENT

AS they say in Chinese: "He who has tasted the bitterness of bitter will be the man of man."

Hence, as always, I am grateful to all those bosses and colleagues whom I have had worked with previously, and who had so kindly inducted me into the web of corporate "intrigues" that I have grown to become more "street smart" from the naive and hapless greenhorn I once was.

Of course, I am also grateful to my wife, Judy, who has always been so steadfast in standing by my side and believing in me, particularly during those bad times when every battle had seemed lost.

PREFACE

THE SUCCESS OF my other books on the application of Sun Tzu's *Art of War* to modern-day management has been reflected in the increased demand for my public and in-house seminars. At these talks, there have been occasions when I was caught by surprise on being introduced as "... an expert in the *Art of War*" or "... a scholar whose works have made him a contemporary interpreter of Sun Tzu".

I am, however, neither an expert nor a scholar. I have always shied off the term 'expert' ever since I was told of its definition—that an expert is "someone who comes out, finds out, tells out, and then gets out before he is found out". As for being a scholar, I believe I am far more pragmatic. As a journalist once wrote: "The first in Southeast Asia to link Sun Tzu's words to business in a 1989 book entitled *War At Work*, Penang-born Mr Khoo is known to take a more practical approach to Sun Tzu's principles, applying them to business with examples culled from his 15 years in management." Similarly, when my other book, *Sun Tzu and Management*, was first reviewed in *Malaysian Business* (November 1-15, 1992), the writer observes: "While doing just that (interpreting Sun Tzu's *Art of War* to contemporary management) may deter many from reading the book, believing it to be nothing but academic pedantry, Khoo has managed to bring the whole subject to a most welcomed level of realism by injecting examples of actual management situations he has come across in his career ..."

And these comments have summed up the situation exactly—I am just a manager, something far from being an expert or a scholar. But rather, closer to home when all we are talking about are really about business and the corporate 'battlefields' which perhaps explains why my writings and my talks found so much popularity among businessmen and executives, who in Sun Tzu's era, would be the rulers and generals.

And like ancient times where court intrigues could destroy a general's career regardless of his valor or strategic brilliance on the battlefields (e.g. the well-known saga of patriotic General Yue Fei of the Sung Dynasty who was recalled, framed by treacherous ministers, and subsequently put to death), today's managers may yet find their careers plagued by negative corporate politicking.

While I too have personally suffered from negative politicking in my time, fortunately, I could always find solutions in Sun Tzu's *Art of War*. Some executives could always turn to their mentors in the company they worked for. But for those who lack a mentor or the creativity to understand, interpret and apply the principles found in Sun Tzu's war principles, to guide them in this aspect of corporate life, I hope this book would be helpful.

Khoo Kheng-Hor
August 1995

INTRODUCING SUN TZU AND THE *ART OF WAR*

WHAT HAS a 2,500-year-old Chinese military strategist to do with corporate politics?

The answer: Plenty. The war principles found in Sun Tzu's *Art of War* has much in common with the present-day aim of acquiring power and influencing people at work so as to do a better and more effective job.

To understand the man and his work, it is appropriate to narrate the following story which is familiar to many Chinese—and an even greater number of Japanese. Around 500BC, when Sun Tzu, a native of Qi, wrote the *Art of War*, Prince He-lu of Wu was so impressed by what he read that he granted him an audience.

The Prince, who had read all of Sun Tzu's thirteen chapters on warfare, wanted to test Sun Tzu's skill in drilling troops, using women. Sun Tzu was prepared to face this test and Prince He-lu sent for 180 ladies from his palace.

Sun Tzu divided them into two companies, each headed by one of the Prince's two favorite concubines. After arming all the women with spears, Sun Tzu asked: "Do you know where is front and back, right and left?"

When all the women replied in the affirmative, Sun Tzu went on to instruct them thus: "When I command 'front', you must face directly ahead; 'turn left', you must face to the left; 'turn right', you must face to the right; 'back', you must turn right around towards your back."

As all the women assented, Sun Tzu laid out the executioner's weapons to show his seriousness regarding discipline, and began the drill to the sounds of drumbeats and shouts of commands. None of the women moved. Instead, they burst into laughter.

Sun Tzu patiently told them that commands which are unclear and, therefore, not thoroughly understood, would be the commander's fault, and proceeded to instruct them once more.

When the drums were beaten a second time and the commands repeated, the women again burst into fits of laughter. This time, Sun Tzu said: "Commands which are unclear and not thoroughly understood would be the commander's fault. But when commands are clear and the soldiers nonetheless do not carry them out, then it is the fault of their officers." So saying, he ordered both concubines who were heading the two companies out for execution.

The Prince, who was witnessing the drill from a raised pavilion, on seeing his favorite concubines sent out for execution, was greatly alarmed and quickly sent an aide with the message: "I believe the general is capable of drilling troops. Without these two concubines, my food and drink will be tasteless. It is my desire that they be spared."

Sun Tzu replied that having received the royal commission to lead troops in the field, he can disregard any of the Ruler's commands as he sees fit. Accordingly, he had the two concubines beheaded as an example and thereafter appointed two women next in line to take their place as company leaders.

Thereafter, the drill proceeded smoothly with every women obediently turning left, right, front or back; kneeling or rising, with perfect precision, without laughing or uttering any dissent.

Sun Tzu then sent a messenger to the Prince requesting him to inspect the troops which he declared as having been properly drilled and disciplined, and prepared even to go through fire and water for the Prince.

When the Prince declined, Sun Tzu remarked: "The Prince is only fond of words which he cannot put into practice."

Greatly ashamed by what he had heard, and recognizing Sun Tzu's ability, Prince He-lu promptly appointed Sun Tzu as the supreme commander of the Wu armies.

In 506BC, Sun Tzu led five expeditions against the State of Zhu which had regarded Wu as a vassal. He defeated the armies of Zhu and forced his way into the Zhu capital, Ying-du, while King Zhao fled, leaving his State on the verge of extermination.

And for almost twenty years thereafter, the armies of Wu continued to be victorious against those of its neighbors, the States of Qi, Qin and Yue. However, after Sun Tzu's death, his successors failed to follow his precepts and suffered defeat after defeat until 473BC when the kingdom became extinct.

PART I

CORPORATE POLITICS
IN PERSPECTIVE

"The general who understands war is the arbiter of the people's fate, and on him depends whether the nation shall be at peace or in danger."

1

THE NATURE OF
CORPORATE POLITICS

WHEN IT COMES to the topic of corporate politics, many executives, including CEOs, have the tendency to emulate the famed ostrich in trying, albeit in vain, to bury its head in the sand.

THE HYPOCRISY

This subject is hence rather taboo in most organizations where in seeking to look good professionally, everyone joins in the pretense that there is no such phenomenon as politicking. Corporate politics is thus given a negative connotation right from the start with the inevitable result that almost everyone pretends politicking does not exist, or if there is politicking of any sort, then the conclusion is reached: the management must be doing a terribly lousy job. No wonder then that no management cares to admit to the existence of corporate politics.

I have even been warned by well-meaning friends and colleagues against writing this book lest I become the object of criticism and ridicule as 'a detestable political animal', 'crazy for power', etc. They even ventured to say that nobody would admit to reading this book even if they are when interviewed by any journalist for the 'Who's reading what?' columns which some newspapers carry.

But this only shows how much people enjoy deceiving themselves. So long as there are people interacting with one another, with each individual and (or) group pursuing interests in divergence with those of other individuals and (or) groups, some kind of politicking almost always results.

THE NECESSITY

A more practical and realistic approach is to recognize the existence of corporate politics and understand its nature to realize that politicking is not necessarily bad but could instead be good. By this, I offer an alternative to the negative side of corporate politics. Seen in a more positive angle, corporate politics can be utilized as *the* mean to get on, become influential and rise up the corporate ladder yet without having to sacrifice our principles and morals to turn into 'super creeps'.

I would even venture to say that politicking is a necessity because to be effective is not just about high performance but is also about being political. From Sun Tzu's *Art of War*, I have come to realize that power, influence, and internal and external politics can be legitimate methods for people seeking success, to increase their personal worth to their organizations by getting the right things done the right way, and thus speed up their climb on the corporate ladder. In his words:

> "In war, what matters is victory, not prolonged
> campaigns. And therefore, the general who understands
> war is the arbiter of the people's fate, and on him
> depends whether the nation shall be at peace or in
> danger."

Peace or danger, like success or failure, will always depend on how we go about approaching our objectives. While working harder, believing in yourself, and positive thinking, may be useful attributes, they are still not enough. My advice then is to be political to get on and get things done.

TERRITORIALITY

However, to appreciate the necessity of politicking, we must first understand its nature. Let us then turn to the work of zoologists who have long ago found evidence of territorial instinct in animals. An example is the male hippopotamus which marks out its territory by defecating all around its perimeter. Should any other hippopotamus enter the territory so marked, it will mean a fight to the death.

Basically, humans being animals themselves, have also got the same territorial instinct although their positioning at the highest level of the animal species, allows their actions to be less crude. We may not actually defecate around us to mark out our territories but we nonetheless have a natural tendency to indicate our possessions, e.g. when moving into new offices, we would use personal items, like calendars, framed photographs, paintings, or college plaques, to decorate our walls, and favorite books to line our shelves, etc. Such actions are tantamount to marking our territories, i.e. "this is my office."

Territorial instinct can also surface when we are in close proximity with others. This is the physical aspect where some people may be more territorially conscious that should you get too near to them, they may actually feel your presence more keenly and show their resentment to such 'intrusion' through body languages like crossing their arms or legs and at times even to the extent of putting up physical objects like a handbag between the two of you (again, a way of saying: "keep off, this is my territory.") or shifting away from you.

TERRITORIAL 'POWER PLAYS'

Territoriality is thus the root of politicking since it arises as a desire to protect our interests. Whether as section heads, department heads, or division heads, we are bound to get involved more or less in territorial 'power plays' when those working with us start behaving in territorial ways. Sometimes we may be the ones who initiated such 'power plays' with others.

Take this example of a territorial 'power play': a director announced an important meeting in *his* office at 2.00 p.m. to decide whether to go ahead with a vital project which had fallen behind schedule. Within the hour, another director who was involved in the project, replied: "Sorry, I cannot make it as I have other urgent appointments already lined up. I could, however, find some time, say at 3.30 p.m., if you could arrange for everyone to meet at *my* office." At about 3.00 p.m., the intercom lines got busy again as frantic secretaries tried to reschedule the meeting to 5.00 p.m. at the first director's office because an 'emergency' had come up for the first director who was so 'tied up that he won't be able to leave his desk'.

So we find each director trying to assert his own importance and (or) demonstrate his dominance over the other by wanting the meeting to be his call and in his office, i.e. territory. No wonder the project was far behind schedule.

Once it is understood that the underlying desire is to protect one's interest, we can see that politicking is very often triggered off by a sense of insecurity. Having understood this, we can start by feeling for the other party and thus use such knowledge to avoid negative consequences and better still, to build closer and more positive rapport in our interactions with others.

WHY WRITE THIS BOOK?

This is my main purpose for writing this book, where I seek to warn you against using self-seeking 'power plays' which could endanger both your position and your friendships. As the great strategist cautioned:

> "One who does not thoroughly understand the calamity
> of war shall be unable to thoroughly comprehend the
> advantage of war."

Instead, I wish to interest you on how you can constructively use his war principles to play corporate politics and be a powerful person at work without 'killing' off the rest. His words of wisdom as contained in the *Art of War* which set me off in this quest, were:

> "Fighting to win one hundred victories in one hundred battles is not the supreme skill. To break the enemy's resistance without fighting is the supreme skill ... The skilful general subdues the enemy's army without fighting. He captures cities without laying siege and overthrows the enemy's reign without protracted campaigns ... This offensive strategy is that of 'using the sheathed sword'."

So you see, politicking does not have to be bad, such as being machiavellian and underhanded. It can be positive as you shall find out for yourself.

故善戰者
能為不可勝
不能使敵必可勝
不可勝在己　可勝在敵

"Invincibility lies in one's own hands but the enemy's vulnerability is of his own making. Thus, those skilled in war can make themselves invincible but the enemy's vulnerability is provided only by the enemy himself."

2

POWER IN ORGANIZATIONS

LIKE CORPORATE POLITICS, power is also viewed by many executives (this time, most CEOs excluded) as something just a little better than an obscene word.

THE MISCONCEPTION

In their wariness of power, many executives see it as a 'necessary evil', i.e. something which you need to wield over others to get them to do things for you. Some even go as far as to denounce power as a distasteful weapon used only by those people who are without integrity, hence the derogatory term, 'power-crazy'.

These are unfortunate misconceptions. Like corporate politics, power can be a positive force which equips a person with the choice, freedom and strength to get things done or even to change things.

In Sun Tzu's era, when China was divided into several warring States, power is something to be desired if one seeks to preserve his State from destruction or being enslaved by another. Speaking in terms of military strength, Sun Tzu says:

"The way of fighting is: if our force is ten times the enemy's, then surround him; five times his, attack him; if double his strength, divide our force into two to be used as 'alternate strategy'; if only equal to his, we must concentrate our force to fight him. When our casualties increase, withdraw. If our force is so much weaker than our enemy's, we should totally avoid him, for if a small army is stubborn, it will only end up being captured by the larger enemy force."

Even then, power also carries certain responsibility because, according to Sun Tzu:

"To win battles and make conquests and to take over all the subjects, but failing to rebuild or restore the welfare of what he gains would be a bad sign, so-called 'wasteful stay' ... Do not act unless it is in the interest of the State. Do not use your troops unless you can win. Do not fight unless you are in danger."

Thus, if you have the power to influence events and make decisions, you need to ensure all these are done with the good of others in mind, and not merely for your own gain.

WITHOUT POWER

Think what will happen if you do not have power. Say, you are a department head and you have just submitted your proposals to your boss in the belief that these proposals are necessary for your organization's survival. But then, the heads of other departments also have their own ideas which they too have proposed to your boss. In the end, even though you may be absolutely right in your proposals, your boss may put your proposals aside because you are not powerful and influential enough.

The scenario now changes: you have been hankering for that promotion for a long time already. Just when you thought you are ready and qualified (you have even pursued higher qualifications through night classes), somebody else got it.

Many executives who are caught in similar situations as described above usually end up saying things like: "I'm no longer going to care. It's all politics. From now on, I'll just concentrate on my work and get on with it." Or worse: "I'm not going to bother to contribute anymore. It's all politics. So I'll just switch off and let others get on with it."

If you have been through any of these set-backs and reacted accordingly, think again. This sort of behavior, i.e. choosing not to get involved, is only for losers— those who either lack the skills or intelligence, or just simply do not have the stomach for the fight. Such naive behavior is only an evasion of responsibility and does not help the organization or those who depend on you. It is therefore not surprising that people lower down in the hierarchy, who watch the behavior of their managers, may not be that inspired in the end. No wonder then that Sun Tzu attributes failure on the part of the troops to poor commanders:

> "When troops are inclined to flee, insubordinate against commands, distressed, disorganized or defeated, it is the fault of the general as none of these calamities arises from natural causes."

GO FOR POWER

On the basis of my argument so far, my advice is: should you feel you have got something worthwhile to offer, and want to contribute towards a healthy future for your organization, then go for power. Learn to acquire power and influence, and of course, how to use them in order that your contribution can be accepted.

Remember the movie, *Patton*? There was a memorable scene where actor George C. Scott playing the general's role, told the assembled troops: "Now I want you to remember that no bastard ever won a war by dying for his country. He won it by making the other poor dumb bastard die for his country."

General Patton (1885-1945) was right— soldiers will only be doing a dis-service to their countries by allowing the enemy troops to kill them instead of the other way around. Similarly, on the corporate 'battlefields', you would not be of any use at all to your organizations by merely being passive in submitting to the will of others. Where are your ideas which you, as a professional executive, are supposed to contribute?

My message here is very clear and straightforward: by shunning politics and power, you are only putting yourself at the mercy of other powerful and influential people and may thus deprive yourself of the involvement in the decision-making process to make things happen and (or) bar yourself from many desirable plum jobs up there. How apt then is the following of Sun Tzu's sayings:

"Invincibility lies in one's own hands but the enemy's
vulnerability is of his own making. Thus, those skilled
in war can make themselves invincible but the enemy's
vulnerability is provided only by the enemy himself."

So who is there to blame if you do not have the desire to make yourself strong by seeking power? There is no point in complaining that it is all politics and conflict when you could reset your attitude more positively towards accepting that they are here to stay and you might just as well learn to deal with them. And remember, a manager can never manage effectively if he does not use power.

SOURCES OF POWER

What then is power? Two researchers, French and Raven have provided a useful framework in classifying the five sources of power. Taken in the light of Sun Tzu's observations, it is a marvel that human behavior is still very much the same today despite the span of some 2,500 years already.

Legitimate Power

This is the power base traditionally associated with a person's formal position in the organization's hierarchy. As Sun Tzu observes:

> "In war, the general first receives his commands from the ruler. He then assembles his troops and blends them into a harmonious entity before pitching camp."

Without having received his commands from the ruler, no general can assemble troops. Similarly, no executive can start managing without having received his appointment. As the position allows one the access to power, it is no wonder that this source is also called position power. Hence, when a manager is appointed to take charge of, say, the finance department, the departmental staff will obey his work instructions only because they perceive this appointment as a legal delegation of formal authority over them.

However, real power does not necessarily rest in letters of appointment, documents and memoranda spelling out the terms of reference and areas of jurisdiction. It lies more in what a person can achieve in practice which means he can still find himself without access to the power which his position ought to carry. Thus, a new manager who has yet to earn the respect of his staff or, for some reasons, have lost their respect, may still find that he is unable to influence them in changing their attitudes or behaviors. This is why Sun Tzu cautions:

> "Secure the loyalty of your troops first before punishing them or they will not be submissive."

It is crazy the way some managers start acting autocratically with their staff the moment they take up their appointments.

Their famous words often take these forms: "You do as I say"; "I don't care ..."; "You're the boss or I'm the boss?" etc.

Reward Power

As seen earlier, we cannot merely rely on our position alone. Exercising legitimate power by itself is still insufficient for control. We must actively seek to motivate the willingness of others in accepting our influence. As Sun Tzu says:

> "Bestows rewards without regard to customary rules ..."

and also his emphasis on rewards,

> "In battle, those who captures more than ten chariots from the enemy must be rewarded ..."

and

> "When plundering the countryside and capturing new lands, divide the profits among your men ..."

and also,

> "... with well-fed troops, await hungry ones."

Our employees must believe we are in the position to reward them for their efforts. Thus, we must be seen to have access to the resources, i.e. in possession of a "bag of goodies", from which to reward them. Such rewards may be the authority to hand out favorable job assignments, promotions, pay increases, bonuses, etc. Since one must have ample resources to be able to hand out rewards, this power base is also referred to as resource power.

Coercive Power

This power-base works on fear which means our employees must believe we are capable of punishing them. Such punishments may take the form of official reprimands, less desirable work assignments, holding out on pay increases, cutting bonuses, taking disciplinary actions such as demotion or even dismissal.

However, do take note of Sun Tzu's caution on the use of punishment:

> "Too frequent punishments show him [the general] to be in dire distress as nothing else can keep them [his men] in check. If the officers at first treat their men harshly and later fear them, then the limit of indiscipline is reached."

Studies of convicts found that some who have grown accustomed to frequent sentencing in their early years for petty offenses may become so hardened that stiff penalties for more serious crimes in later years may no longer deter them from breaking the law. The same applies to the workplace where an employee, if punished too often, the punishment process tends to lose its effect and the behavior of the errant employee could deteriorate for the worse. And when the manager responsible for such an employee begins to fear him, chaos would inevitably follow.

Expert Power

This power-base is not the monopoly of the management but is also accessible to the rank-and-file members of an organization. When a person possesses a special knowledge or skill which is acutely needed, he is said to wield expert power. However, expert power tends to be narrow in scope because knowledge or skill is limited only to specific task areas.

I know a computer whiz-kid who works in an organization which started using a new complicated software. He was very much in demand in the initial stages when everyone clamored for his assistance and advice since he was then the only one in the organization familiar with the particular software. Department heads who used to chide him for his long-winded nature, suddenly became very meek and patient with him during those early months as they tried to learn as much as they can from him. For a few months, he found he wielded much power over these people, but once the computerization finally sank in, he realized he no longer carry the same clout as before.

Sun Tzu, however, warns:

"When the common soldiers are stronger than their officers, they will insubordinate. When the officers are too strong and the troops are weak, the result is collapse."

To be effective in his job, a person must know more about his job than what his staff knows. Supposing you have just joined a firm as a sales manager, and you found out that your assistant knows more about your company's products, customers, competitors, etc., than you do. This is bound to create some problems in your working relationship with him sooner or later. This has contributed to turnover of capable staff in some organizations. Another problem of having too highly knowledgeable or skilled employees is that of the organization being held to ransom by the said employees.

On the other hand, it is just as bad to have a manager who is so much more advanced and dynamic in ideas and actions than his staff who would always be lagging far behind him. Although the staff may be fairly good employees in terms of intelligence and diligence, having a super-intelligent and super-diligent boss can also create problems in their working relationship. For example, on the principle of relativity, the boss may unfairly appraise his staff as simply incompetent.

Referent Power

Sometimes a person may do something for you, not because you are his superior who order him to do so, or able to reward or punish him, but simply because he feels a strong attachment to or identifies with you. This source of power which is often based on personal admiration means employees find some admirable personal characteristics, charisma, or good reputation in their bosses. Sun Tzu has this to say:

> "Such a general who protects his soldiers like infants will have them following him into the deepest valleys. A general who treats his soldiers like his own beloved sons will have their willingness to die for him."

This is a fundamental principle: Treat your employees with respect and fairness and they will reciprocate in turn.

From the above power sources, you can see that power is indeed part and parcel of our daily corporate activities. How then can we truly say we do not care for power and has no use for it? Remember those are the words of losers who, in their haplessness, ought not be in the corporate 'battlefields' in the first place. While we should not abuse our power, we should still develop it and use it lest it will be someone else making the decisions and he may not be right. It pays then to recall what Sun Tzu has written so long ago:

> "Thus, the general who advances without coveting fame and withdraws without fearing disgrace, but whose sole intention is to protect the people and serve his ruler, is the precious jewel of the State."

Always remember, as a professional, you owe your subordinates and the other employees in the organization (not forgetting your employers), the obligation to do your best, and shirking your responsibility to push your best idea or ideas across, is certainly *not* doing your best.

知彼知己
勝乃不殆
知天知地
勝乃不窮

"Know your enemy, know yourself and your victory will be undoubted. Know Earth and Heaven and your victory will be complete."

3

THE CORPORATE CULTURE

AN ANCIENT SAYING which is often quoted in the Chinese classical novel, *Romance of the Three Kingdoms*, goes like this: "Like the clever bird which chooses the right branch to perch, the wise servant will choose the right master to serve."

GETTING IT RIGHT FROM THE START

In line with this saying, it is essential that one chooses wisely and joins the right corporation, right from the start. Even if you are an expert in the *Art of War*, you will still fail if you do not start off right. This could be what Sun Tzu has in mind when he first wrote: "One may know how to win and yet is unable to do it." As such, many executives have found their careers stagnated or even ruined just because they had joined the wrong organizations.

It is very important then that one must carefully and wisely choose the 'battlefield' that one wishes to fight on, for as Sun Tzu cautions:

> "There are some roads which we must not follow; some enemy troops we must not fight; some cities we must not attack; some grounds we must not contest; even some orders from the ruler which we must not obey."

Selecting the right 'battlefield' to fight involves the following priorities: knowing what you want, i.e. the job you would like to do; the type of working environment which suits you best; and of course, finding out more about the organization you wish to join, especially in terms of its 'heaven' which Sun Tzu has defined as follows:

> "By heaven, I mean the working of natural forces; the effects of winter's cold and summer's heat, and the conduct of military operations according to the seasons."

In this context, I would interpret his 'heaven' to be the organization climate or the corporate culture.

CORPORATE CULTURE

Many modern-day writers have attempted to define corporate culture which in a nutshell, could be summed up simply as a complex set of assumptions, beliefs, perceptions, symbols and values that define the way in which an organization goes about conducting its business. In this way, corporate culture can greatly influence the choice of goals, policies and strategies in an organization. Serious differences could lead to clashes if you try to get people to do things that are counter to their beliefs and values. It is essential then that the culture must appeal to your nature. This is what Sun Tzu has to say:

> "Conformation of the terrain is the soldier's best ally in battle."

Take the corporate culture of one US *Fortune-500* company whose critics had described as a 'sharks' culture, i.e. executives in the firm are encouraged by their top management to compete fiercely, not only with their external competitors but also internally amongst themselves. As we know, sharks swim together and hunt together. But should any one of them be unfortunate enough as to cut its belly on the sharp corals down below and start bleeding, the rest will devour it for their next meal.

In the particular firm, it has been said that if one wishes to climb the corporate ladder, he must not only make his colleagues look silly, but also must be prepared to squeeze out his immediate supervisor should the opportunity allow. Actually, we cannot condemn this sort of culture as bad. Each corporation has its own type of culture and the particular one that I have just described, is just the said firm's own way of doing things, and while such a culture may put off certain people, it has yet succeeded in attracting others, particularly those young, ambitious and aggressive graduates.

A good example of a pervasive culture of intense competition is that of PepsiCo where severe pressure is put on managers to show continual improvement in market share, and managers are constantly moved to new jobs, as a result of which employees worked long hours and engaged in political maneuvering just to keep their jobs from being reorganized out from under them. Such a culture has the effect of screening out less competitive managers while keeping those with the competitive values and attitudes that the top PepsiCo management believes are required if their firm is to become number one. Even Sun Tzu also has something to say about this:

> "His [the general's] business is to assemble his troops
> and throw them into critical position. He leads them
> deep into enemy territory to further his plans."

On the other hand, readers of Singapore's *The Straits Times* would have, from time to time, seen Hewlett-Packard's job advertisements featuring pictures of dolphins. Does that not tell you a story about the company? These highly intelligent, lovable and playful creatures are known to swim together, hunt together, but should any of them get injured, the rest would gang up and become most protective in escorting the injured member to safety.

This must be the epitome of 'team spirit' as we have been hearing these days. It is no wonder then that ever since the founding of a strong team commitment at Hewlett-Packard in the 1940s by Bill Hewlett and Dave Packard, the corporation has lived up to its policy that it would not be a 'hire-and-fire' company. This principle was severely tested on a couple of occasions in the 1970s, when slowdown in business forced the company to adopt the policy of a 'nine-day fortnight' whereby staff took a 10 per cent pay cut and worked 10 per cent fewer hours while other companies resorted to layoffs. In this way, like the dolphins, the Hewlett-Packard team showed they share the same fortune and that a measure of job security is possible even in bad times.

A PERSONAL LESSON

As I have said earlier, selecting the right organization is very important. For all your skills in the *Art of War*, you will still fail if you do not start off right.

There was an occasion when I left a dynamic and fast-paced organization to join another which offered me a General Manager's position. I supposed, after having been in a fast-paced organization where I was given virtually total freedom in making decisions and taking responsibility for my actions, it was inevitable that I found it very difficult to adjust to the different culture at the new workplace.

It did not take me too long to find out that my designation as General Manager did not carry as much authority (in terms of decision making) as I would expect or wish to have. Even though four other departmental managers reported to me, the system still requires endorsement by my boss. As I am quite impatient by nature, I felt very chagrined from having to wait for my boss to approve all the things I would like to do. In my inability to come to terms with such a culture which is so different from the ones I had been accustomed to, I did not stay long there.

In retrospect, I must admit that I had committed gross negligence in overlooking one of Sun Tzu's wise sayings:

"Know your enemy, know yourself and your victory
will be undoubted. Know Earth, know Heaven and
your victory will be complete."

Although I know myself well enough, I had failed to find out more about the organization I was joining, especially in terms of its culture and the management style. Had I checked and found out more about the corporate culture of the firm which I was joining, I may not have had joined the company since my temperament and the organization's work system would not match at all. In short, I was not being very smart then.

This is why I must caution you— whether you are a fresh job-seeker or an experienced executive—to be very careful about joining the right corporation or else you will not go very far. Look for a boss that you can relate to because if you like who you are working for, you are going to want to do things naturally. You must have a good idea of who you are working for, so as to put yourself in a position where it works. And of course, next to the boss, also find out as much as possible the environment and its people. But do not accept such information from the Personnel Manager or the boss personally during the job interview. He or she might give you the wrong impression, saying something like: "You will enjoy working here. We have such a good bunch here, no politicking at all."

PART II

POSITIVE POLITICS

"By command, I mean the general's stand for the virtues of wisdom, sincerity, benevolence, courage and strictness."

4

MAKING YOURSELF STRONG

LET US ASSUME that you have decided on what you would like to do, found out all you need to know about the organization you are joining, and satisfied with the matching, are about to settle into your new job. Great, before you go rushing about trying to handle others at your new workplace, learn first to handle yourself, i.e. concentrate on making yourself strong.

BEING INVINCIBLE

As I have quoted Sun Tzu earlier:

> "Invincibility lies in one's own hands but the enemy's vulnerability is of his own making. Thus, those skilled in war can make themselves invincible but the enemy's vulnerability is provided only by the enemy himself."

Put another way, as you are your enemy's enemy, he need not have to make you weak because if you are not careful, you will just create your own vulnerability and provide your own downfall to your enemy's benefit. You should instead be working on your own strengths to become invincible. If you want to know how, let us turn once more to Sun Tzu who says:

> "The good commander seeks virtues and goes about disciplining himself according to the laws so as to effect control over his success."

I take this advice to mean one must exercise self-discipline if one wants to be successful. Nothing comes easy in this world, especially in the corporate world. To get ahead, we sometimes have to do the things which we usually do not like to do, for example, when submitting a report to top management, we may have to put in the extra effort in tapping our network to check out the facts, clock the extra hours to ensure no mistakes, etc.

In this context, we shall need to discipline ourselves to cultivate what Sun Tzu has called the 'five virtues'.

THE FIVE VIRTUES OF A GENERAL
When referring to the term, 'command', Sun Tzu explains:

> "By command, I mean the general's stand for the virtues of wisdom, sincerity, benevolence, courage and strictness."

On Wisdom
To be politically wise, one must always have knowledge, especially what Sun Tzu has called 'foreknowledge':

> "The enlightened ruler and the wise general can subdue the enemy whenever they move and they can achieve superhuman feats because they have foreknowledge."

Such knowledge is not just for knowing what is going on in one's immediate environment but also for reading beyond a situation to comprehend the strategic implications. This can perhaps be summed up in one of Sun Tzu's most famous sayings:

> "If you know yourself and know your enemy; in a hundred battles, you will never fear the result. When you know yourself but not your enemy, your chances of winning or losing are equal. If you know neither

yourself nor your enemy, you are certain to be in danger
in every battle."

Knowledge is indeed the first step to power. And knowledge
can only come from accumulated experience and (or) information gathered from various sources, one of which is networking
which we shall discuss in greater detail in Chapter 9. By far the
easiest way to gather information is to spend 'visiting' time with
both peers and subordinates. This is what contemporary management gurus have called 'management-by-walking-around'.

Ever since I first started out as a Personnel Manager in 1980,
walking, sometimes as long as four hours a day on the factory
grounds of Malayan Sugar Manufacturing Company Berhad in
Prai, Malaysia, had taught me the wisdom of tapping into the informal network. From Sun Tzu, I learned:

"When troops are seen whispering amongst themselves
in small groups, the general has lost the confidence of his
men."

The lesson is to identify the various informal groups at work,
know who the leaders are, and thereafter subtly cultivate these
leaders for information and support for the management. In this
way, I would quietly but aggressively tap the informal leaders
from time to time for information on how their fellow workers
felt and thought about certain policies or the general sentiment
towards their supervisors and (or) managers. That was how on
several occasions in the past I was forewarned before any incident
happened. And sometimes even before implementing any change
at the workplace, I would first 'sell' the concept to these informal
leaders and only after having convinced them, would enlist their
support to thereafter push the change across. This is in keeping
with what Sun Tzu has called 'using direct and indirect methods':

"Generally, in battle, use the direct methods to engage
the enemy forces; indirect methods are however needed
to secure victory."

The direction from my bosses or my initiative as a manager
to implement a change is the 'direct' approach while using the
key informal leaders to forward my plans is the 'indirect' approach. In return for their support, I would accommodate their
occasional small requests, e.g. change of shift duties, time-off, or
installation of amenities such as fans, hot water system, etc.

And for any newcomer to an organization, it pays to be sensitive to the environment and the people. If I were to quote Sun
Tzu, it would be:

"Those who do not know the conditions of mountains,
forests, high and dangerous grounds, defiles, marshes,
and swamps, cannot conduct the march of an army."

and

"That you may march a thousand *li* (one *li* = half mile)
without exhaustion is due to the country being free of
enemy troops."

Be free of enemies by being unobtrusive. When you start a
new job, take it easy. People do not know you well enough as yet
to trust you. And do not try to be too clever, such as setting yourself up as an expert right away. This could only make you unpopular as people could only accept your expertise only after you
have proved yourself in the new organization and not before.

On Sincerity

A basic platform of sincerity is to try to see the good in people.
While we should not be so naive as to think everyone is a saint,

we should refrain from viewing our opponents as enemies. See them simply as people who need more convincing than others. With this attitude in place, start working on your communication skill so that you could explain things properly and tactfully to ensure they come around and share your views. I have found that most people can actually be helpful and co-operative if we take the time and trouble to approach them right.

In this way, I also view sincerity as having an openness with all those we deal with so that they not only know their views matter but also where they stand when dealing with us.

Hence, with regards the information which I got from those informal leaders whose friendships and trusts I have always sought to cultivate, I would use them either to check if there has been any misinterpretation of my intention so as to set things right or to help other supervisors and (or) managers get their situations in order. My sincerity has been proven all these years in that I have never used such information to victimize anyone and I keep strict confidence on the identity of my sources (I learned this from my journalism days). Should anyone use such information to victimize or be indiscreet, he would not only be most insincere but would also be unwise since no one would thereafter offer any information. This must be why Sun Tzu says:

"The confidentiality given to secret operations is greater than for other matters. Only the one who is wise and sagely, benevolent and just, can use secret agents. Only he who is sensitive and subtle can get the truth of their reports."

However, in being sincere, we should not be overly carried away by baring all. Even Sun Tzu has cautioned:

"Do not let your enemy understand the plans concerning your troop movement."

and also

"He [the general] changes his arrangements and alters
his plans so that no one knows what he is up to."

A Sales Manager heard through his key informants that certain salesmen were agitating the others to protest against their sales quotas. He immediately called for a meeting to clarify certain points which he might have failed to convey clearly during the previous meeting. Though this meeting could have succeeded in convincing the majority that the quotas were fair and sound, he ended up losing credibility because in the process, he named those who had tipped him off. To protect themselves, they vehemently denied and suggested that he was attempting the 'divide-and-rule' strategy on the sales teams. Later, when asked why he mentioned the names as he did, he replied: "I thought I should be sincere in the meeting and lay open all my cards."

On Benevolence

Like politicians seeking to project a kindly image to build goodwill amongst voters in their constituents, being benevolent in corporate politics is simply about caring and showing kindness towards one's subordinates and other employees. Although a strict disciplinarian, Sun Tzu advocated on a couple of occasions:

"Treat your men kindly but keep strict control over
them to ensure victory."

and

"A general who protects his soldiers like infants will
have them following him into the deepest valleys. A
general who treats his soldiers like his own beloved sons
will have their willingness to die for him."

People of high status tend to establish and maintain their power by being responsive to requests for their help and time. This can result in reciprocity so that high-status people, through their generosity, actually end up helping themselves. Sometimes such a 'helping hand' is voluntary and not upon request. Moreover, the generosity can be offered to anyone beyond one's immediate circle.

As an extension of sincerity, it has always been my style to show concern for not only my staff but also other employees. I would remember birthdays and thereafter send a personal handwritten card to whoever is concerned, attend funerals and offer condolences, send congratulatory messages on their weddings or promotions, etc. I will also try to assist (within my means, of course) all those who would seek my assistance or even offering such assistance. In this way, I work hard to build goodwill within my immediate circle and beyond.

On Courage

It always take courage to say 'no' because most people usually tend to worry about causing offense or would feel guilty for having to deny others of their requests. Any executive who cannot say 'no' would, however, soon become overloaded and ineffective.

It takes even more courage to say 'no' to bosses. A friend of mine who started off using the same strategy as mine to cultivate informal leaders to get information, was asked by his boss to reveal his sources. Despite knowing his boss was one man who could not keep confidence and had a reputation for harboring malice against those who spoke out against him, my friend still told him. As a result, two of the key informal leaders were subsequently victimized. No one blamed the boss but everyone started avoiding my friend thereafter. He did not stay long in the organization.

Then there was a Personnel Manager who, during a meeting, was directed by her Managing Director to issue a circular prohibiting employees from taking evening courses. She did not even try to point out that after work, employees could jolly well do what they please with their own time. For her lack of courage to say 'no' to her boss, she has lost much respect of her colleagues and the other employees whom she is supposed to take care of. If only more people could read and really dare to apply the following of Sun Tzu's sayings:

> "If the situation offers victory but the ruler forbids
> fighting, the general may still fight. If the situation is
> such that he cannot win, then the general must not fight
> even if the ruler orders him to do so."

One must thus have the courage to speak up. But what is not so apparent is that one must also have the courage to accept criticisms. Most people resent being criticized and when they find criticisms coming their way, the natural tendency is to rationalize them off. For this reason, the more power you have, the more difficult it is to get your subordinates who are the most affected by your managerial behavior, to tell you how and where you have gone wrong. The only remedy, of course, is your willingness to listen, accept or explain, without wanting to get back at the informant or source. As such is very hard to do, it is no wonder that essential feedback usually dries up as one moves higher up the corporate ladder.

On Strictness (or Discipline)

To start off, let me repeat this piece of advice from Sun Tzu who says:

"The good commander seeks virtues and goes about disciplining himself according to the laws so as to effect control over his success."

Here, we could start by being strict about our looks, personal grooming and how we carry ourselves. You will not win confidence if you go around wearing a worried look or dragging your feet when you walk, or being tongue-tied and dare not speak up when spoken to, or when you do, you gesture nervously or have a shaky voice. All these could make others perceive you as indecisive or insecure. So, stop having that 'beaten dog' look on your face, smile your best, and start cultivating confidence. My wife have always insisted that I walk straight with purposeful strides and when I sit, to remember to keep my back up straight because far too many people let their status fade when they slouch into an easy chair. With confidence, half the battle is usually won.

Sun Tzu could not have been closer to the truth when he observes:

"One who foresees victory before a battle will most probably win. One who predicts not much of a chance of winning before a fight, will most probably not win."

and

"He wins by making no mistake. Making no mistake means already having established the certainty of victory; conquering an enemy who is already defeated."

So do not make the mistake of believing that 'clothes don't maketh a man'. How you dress and what you wear are just as important. I have learned from experience that whenever I fell ill, I should refrain from lazing about my bed in my pajamas with unwashed and unshaved face. That will only make me feel worse.

Instead, if I were to force myself up (and this takes discipline), wash and shave, take a shower, and change into fresh clothes, and only then rest as the doctor has ordered, I tend to feel better.

Very often, people would judge you by what you wear. That was why my late father, in his lifetime, would insist on all his sons and daughters wearing Rolex watches. In his words: "It's an investment. Even if it costs you $10,000 a piece, if you were to wear it for 10 years, that would work to something like only $2.74 a day. And the facts are, it may last you a lifetime and chances are, it could earn you some respect as others may perceive you as having made it." Hence, while you should be disciplined in not living beyond your means, you should also be disciplined in developing a strategic mind to invest in your image.

The next step in cultivating self-discipline is to lead by example. This means you must be a person of your word. Start with the small issues, such as keeping appointments and honoring commitments and promises. And make sure, when you assign a task on someone else, you are personally capable and willing to do that task yourself.

A GENERAL'S FIVE DANGEROUS FAULTS
In his wisdom, Sun Tzu could see that man is fallible and hence he warns:

> "There are five dangerous faults which a general should not have in his character. Recklessness leads to destruction; cowardice ends in capture; quick temper enables you to make him look foolish; delicate in honor causes sensitivity to shame; overly compassionate for his men exposes him to worries and harassment. These five faults in a general can seriously ruin military operations."

Let us look at each one in turn:

On Recklessness

Much of what our friends and opponents at our workplace tells us, usually would come from their own twisty perspectives. It is therefore wise to seek further information before reacting or setting yourself onto any task. Otherwise, the end results could simply be as Sun Tzu has foreseen:

"When one sets in motion an entire army to chase an advantage, the chances are that he will not attain it."

One day, one of my consultants stormed into my room at 5.30 p.m. and announced: "I'm back. I was actually at our client's office but I *rushed* straight back." The accusing tone tinged with resentment was unmistakable. While keeping a cool facade, my mind raced over a few facts—this lady was generally pleasant and polite; as she had been assigned to handle an executive search exercise, she was supposed to fax over a report to a client that morning; when her manager reported to me at 4.30 p.m. that she had gone out with another consultant to see a client, I said: "But had she faxed over the report to Ms Eng already?" Her manager said she will page her and find out.

Thereafter, I asked the consultant: "So why are you so worked up for?" She replied: "You must understand, I was visiting our client and really doing my job. Then I heard you were angry and wanted me back because you wanted the report faxed over."

I told her it was true that I would expect the fax to be sent that morning itself. And although annoyed, I was not that angry to want her back immediately since she was already out at the client's office. I would only summon her back if it was a matter of life and death. I then called in her manager and the three of us had a face-to-face talk over how the communication process had led to the consultant being so upset. The facts then emerged: her manager read from my annoyance that I *could* be angry and thus took upon herself to caution her to come back.

After that, I cautioned the consultant on the danger of reck-lessness, saying: "Had I been a nasty boss, you could have been booted out of my room quite unceremoniously for storming into my room the way you did." Silently, I also congratulated myself for having learned the virtue of tolerance so as to find out more because had I too been reckless as to boot out the consultant, I could have lost an enthusiastic staff as well as demoralize her col-leagues. As Sun Tzu observes:

> "Hence, the enlightened ruler is prudent and the good general should not be hasty. Thus a country is safe and the army preserved."

On Cowardice

You can always spot the cowardly ones in any organization. To make up for their lack of courage and to some extent, lack of es-teem, they are often given to bluster and bluff, that is, acting higher than their actual status to their subordinates. In this way, they would often resort to threats of disciplinary action ("Do as I tell you, or I'll ..."). Their behavior would often get worse when they come under pressure from either their peers or bosses or both.

On the other hand, there is a limit to what subordinates can take in terms of punishments or threats of punishment from their superiors. There will come a time when an employee who has been punished or threatened once too often, would insubordi-nate with vehemence. And when such happens, the cowardly na-ture of the superior would usually manifest itself, for as Sun Tzu has observed some 2,500 years ago:

> "Too frequent punishment shows him [the general] to be in dire distress as nothing else can keep the [the soldiers] in check. If the officers at first treat the men

46

harshly and later fear them, the limit of indiscipline is reached."

At such times, you would not only appear hapless to your boss and colleagues but those who are more inclined towards negative politicking may even take this opportunity to show up your incompetence.

On Quick Temper

If temper is your Achilles' heel, then beware of those who would bait you, for this is what Sun Tzu has tried to warn many times:

"If he is prone to choleric temper, irritate him."

and

"... a quick temper, which enables you to make him look foolish."

and again,

"Provoke his agitation and so learn the pattern of his movement."

So you see, your temper could be your own downfall.

I once had a colleague who just cannot keep his cool. All one has got to do is to provoke him and he would just get all heated up and start going on the defensive. It is no wonder then that he was regarded with contempt by everyone as a loser. The lesson here is this: when there is hostility and anger around, the one who stays calm and composed would always hold the power regardless of how abusive the other party is. How appropriate then is Sun Tzu's observation:

"It is the business of a general to be calm and mysterious; fair and composed."

Calmness can only be had if you are able to distance yourself psychologically and avoid engaging in a row. Remember the following Sun Tzu's sayings:

"If the general cannot control his anger and sends his soldiers to swarm up the walls like ants, then one-third of the troops will be killed without taking the city."

and

"No ruler should put troops into the field because he is angry; no general should fight because he is resentful. Move only when there is benefit to be gained, quit when there is no more advantage. For an angry man can later become happy, a resentful man become pleased, but a kingdom once destroyed can never be restored nor the dead be brought back to life."

As most people are inclined to mix facts and emotion in any written or spoken communication, learn to separate the two. Try to understand the problem instead of becoming emotionally involved.

In 1993, shortly after Kentucky Fried Chicken launched a new product called "Creole chicken" in Singapore, I noticed my colleague, the Marketing Director, appearing somewhat unsure as to whether he should hand over a piece of document to me during a break in a meeting. After some hesitation, he finally passed the document to me. It was a store audit report— usually undertaken by our advertising agency after each promotion.

The report informed of random checks done at three stores which found a piece of cold chicken, a piece of chicken with unappetizing glazing, and a piece of chicken which appeared smaller than the advertising shots. But apart from these facts, the report went on to criticize operations severely.

After reading the report, I told my colleague: "Paul, rest assured I will send out another reminder on holding time to ensure products are always warm. As for the improper glazing, looks like we need another round of training for the crew. I will also inform Quality Control to step up the checks on stock input from the suppliers to ensure no under-sized chicken."

I could tell my colleague was impressed by my objectivity in seeking to rectify the problems instead of getting worked up over the critical comments and trying needlessly to defend the situation.

On Delicate in Honor

I have noticed that people tend to be most cautious when feeling out a newcomer to an organization. Some (the more aggressive or mischievous ones) may even put you to a test or two.

Once, after I had joined an organization (whose name I shall withhold to protect the innocent), as part of my orientation program, a schedule was drawn up for the various department heads to meet and brief me on their functions. As I was a senior executive, all except one came promptly to my office during the appointed time. When the culprit failed to turn up after a fifteen-minute wait, I called him. He feigned surprise, claimed he had forgotten as a result of his heavy workload, and then had the temerity to suggest: "Say, why don't *you* come over to *my* office?"

I told him I would. And when I entered his room, I said: "I'm glad you invited me to come over as I have a preference to meet in other people's room." That caused him to raise his eyebrows, and when he asked why, I replied: "First, I like to see your room because it tells me how you work. As a matter of fact, it also tells me your character. And meeting in your room further allows me to decide when I want to end this meeting ... that is, I'll simply take my leave."

I could see he was impressed and thereafter we had a most amicable discussion. In his attempt to bait me, he realized I was no push-over even though I played along. He was even more impressed by the fact that even though I outranked him— I was then a division head while he was head of only a small department— I was not overly sensitive over our status but sportingly took his bait and yet treated him as a respected colleague. As a result, he became one of my allies over the years I was with the company.

On Being Overly Compassionate

As stated earlier, when a general is overly compassionate for his men, he is exposing himself to worry and harassment. And most of these worries are unnecessary.

I once found out that some of the staff in a company I was then heading, could earn more from overtime claims than their normal salary. When I questioned the manager concerned, he admitted he did not actually requested those staff to work overtime. They would simply stay back after office hours, and then submit their claims which he will thereafter approve without checking. His explanation: "What's wrong in helping my staff make some extra income?" That was one Robin Hood who got fired.

In another firm, a manager was simply so sweet and nice to her staff that whenever they misconstrued the company's policies or aired their grievances (even unfounded ones), she would just smile sweetly and promise sincerely to take up the issues on their behalf with top management. When I later took her to task on her team's indiscipline, she insisted that it is her basic nature to be kind which prompted me to point out that by being overly compassionate, she has ceased to behave like a professional manager but was merely being a messenger girl. As she could not comprehend what I told her about not confusing firmness with unkindness, she did not stay long with me.

Thus, be careful that you do not slip this way. Have the following of the great strategist's words carved into your mind:

> "Treat your men kindly but keep strict control over them to ensure victory."

The message is simply: be firm yet fair.

WINNING WITHOUT FIGHTING

You should have guessed by now what I have been trying to tell you in this chapter. By working to cultivate the five virtues and seeking to eliminate the five dangerous faults, your chances of ending up as a power to be reckoned with at your workplace is very high. As Sun Tzu points out:

> "The skilful general subdues the enemy's army without fighting. He captures cities without laying siege and overthrows the enemy's reign without protracted operations."

This is what Sun Tzu has called, 'using the sheathed sword strategy'. A win-win situation where your bosses, peers, and subordinates respect you and work with you in unison.

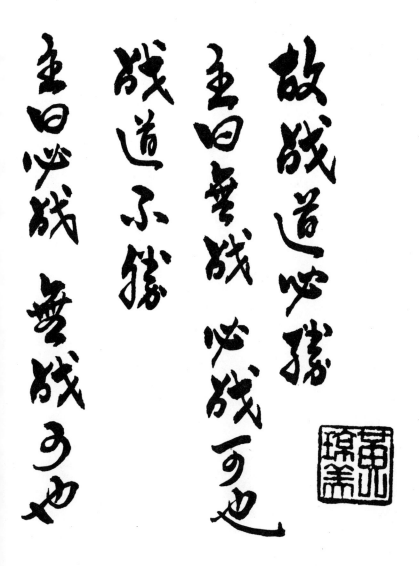

故戰道必勝　主曰無戰　必戰可也

戰道不勝　主曰必戰　無戰可也

"If the situation offers victory but the ruler forbids fighting, the general may still fight. If the situation is such that he cannot win, then the general must not fight even if the ruler orders him to do so."

5

WORKING WITH BOSSES

SINCE MOST executives are more comfortable dealing with those who are below them on the hierarchy than those above, I will discuss this more difficult topic first.

THE EXTREMES

Your boss could be of your own choice on one hand, or simply someone forced upon you on the other. It is easier to handle if it is the former since the chances are that you would have already found out all you can about him. The latter situation is far more trickier as the situation could very well be beyond your control since it could be due to a re-organization or restructuring where someone is brought into your firm from outside, or worse, your firm has been taken over by another company whose management is intent on placing their own people in key positions.

WORKING WITH BOSSES OF YOUR CHOICE

Some useful principles are:

Don't underestimate your boss

If your boss is of your choice, then I take it that you have followed the principles contained in Chapter 3 earlier, e.g. found out in advance about your boss's management style. And having joined him, start getting to know him better (i.e. confirm he is what you have been told about) and at the same time, let him know you better too. And do this as far as possible, in an open manner, not in a manipulative way because it is never wise to assume that your boss is an idiot and could be manipulated. As Sun Tzu warns:

> "But anyone who lacks consideration and treats the enemy with contempt and disdain will only end up being captured."

So think again if you regard your boss as a fool. You may end up the foolish one instead.

When his company was weakened by competitors poaching some of his colleagues away, a key manager tried to manipulate his boss into adjusting his salary by dropping hints that he too had been approached with offers of higher pay. When his boss did nothing, he tendered his resignation (even though he has not yet secured another job) and that led to his boss's immediate decision—to sell off the company!

Put yourself in your boss's shoes

One way of fostering closer working relationship is to put yourself in your boss's shoes. This is what Sun Tzu has advised:

> "As water shapes its flow according to the ground, an army wins by relating to the enemy it faces."

Stop seeing things only from your viewpoint. There are far too many executives who would say things like: "I'm great at my job if only my boss stops interfering, I'm sick of him" or "My boss is such a pain, he's always putting off the decisions I'm trying to get from him." While it is true that there are many bad bosses in existence, still let us try to be more objective and ask ourselves truthfully whether it is really our bosses' faults or our own shortcomings to be blamed. If we made an effort, we may perhaps find that bosses could also be constrained by the limits to their power and thus may not be able to do what we want every time. As such, the more we understand our boss's pressures, needs and ambitions, the more easily we will be able to work well with him.

Plan ahead and develop a 'strategic' mindset

Middle-level managers will especially need to plan their approach in gaining their bosses' acceptance of their proposals through taking a more strategic view of the business. A common complaint from top managers is that middle managers are unable to grasp the larger picture and (or) not accepting the need to balance short-term and long-term implications. Take a cue from Sun Tzu then:

> "More planning shall give greater possibility of victory while less planning, lesser possibility of victory. So how about totally without planning? By this measure, I can clearly foresee victory or defeat."

As a general rule-of-thumb, all bosses dislike half-baked ideas which is why anything you do, should be thoroughly planned so that your boss can see you as a competent, prudent and trustworthy person. Planning, at middle management level, will involve the total organization and not just part of it. This is how any top manager will view any business decision. Thus, if you are trying to win over your boss's support for your proposal but are basing your arguments solely on the needs and plans of your part of the organization, then the probability of you failing is high because you are not seeing the whole picture as your boss has to. Similarly, keep out the minor issues or irrelevant details as you can always deal with such yourself. What irks most bosses would be subordinates who bring everything— major and minor issues— to their attention.

Have the courage to ask, speak up or take action

And be courageous in raising questions, speaking up or taking action whenever the need arises. This is one common shortcoming of most people as they either stand too much in awe of their bosses who are perceived to have special rights, or believe that if they got on the wrong side of their bosses, the latter will use (or misuse) their power against them. This perhaps explains why there are so many 'yes' men in corporations. How many times have we heard: "If my boss wants me to do something which I know will not work, I'll still do it otherwise he will think I'm not supportive," or "Since my boss is an expert in his field, it is not for me to question his view," or "If I tell my boss what I really think of her idea, I'm sure she'll try to nail me one of these days."

If you could recall what I have quoted earlier of Sun Tzu's words, the great strategist says:

"If the situation offers victory but the ruler forbids fighting, the general may still fight. If the situation is such that he cannot win, then the general must not fight even if the ruler orders him to do so."

And true enough, many bosses actually would like their people to be more truthful. Take Prince He-lu, for example, he could have killed Sun Tzu for executing his two favorite concubines against his wishes (see "Introducing Sun Tzu and the *Art of War*") but instead, he made Sun Tzu the Supreme Commander of his armies.

It thus made my day when John Bowmer, the CEO of Adia Worldwide, told me to feel free to call him anytime, saying: "I won't respect any executive who, by taking my instructions blindly, ended up proving my decision to be a wrong one. I would prefer that he takes it as his responsibility in the first place to convince me that I am wrong *before* we even embark on the project." In the same way, there are many bosses like my immediate regional CEO, John Heaney, who tend to respond favorably to requests, disagreements and discussions so long as these are put across confidently, and at the appropriate time and place.

Once during a meeting, when I was Director of Operations at Kentucky Fried Chicken in Singapore, my boss, Michael Gian, directed me to get my project and operations teams ready to work on the opening of a satellite store at a shopping mall. Notwithstanding that we already have a main store in the complex itself, I was still disturbed over the choice of the intended location. Without openly disagreeing with him (too many people, in trying to undermine their bosses publicly, end up undermining themselves when their bosses hit back), I requested for time to think it over and promised to get back to him soonest. Knowing my style, he did not press the issue. After the meeting, I followed him to his room where we argued out the pros and cons on a one-to-one basis. It was then that I realized his constraints which prompted me to put every effort behind the project.

The point I am trying to stress here is that bosses are also human and respond to the courtesies and thoughtfulness that other humans respond to. Thereafter, and till today, Michael and I are still friends as we have a mutual respect for each other.

Impress your boss on your sincerity

Besides being courageous, you must also be capable of impressing your bosses that you are what Sun Tzu has called, the 'precious jewel of the State':

> "Thus, the general who advances without coveting fame
> and withdraws without fearing disgrace, but whose sole
> intention is to protect the people and do good service for
> his ruler, is the precious jewel of the State."

In 1989, about six weeks after I joined Metroplex Berhad, a Malaysian public-listed corporation, as Personnel and Administration Manager and had demonstrated my competence on the job, my boss, Mrs S.K. Chan, wanted to promote me to Group Personnel and Administration Manager. I protested on the ground that I was then still new, not having completed even my probation period as yet. She pointed out that it was her prerogative as the boss and as such could waive the probation period. I said: "I know you're the boss. But I also have my peers to work with, and it won't do if they think I'm your 'blue-eyed' boy." In the end, we settled for job enlargement with a corresponding re-designation instead of promotion.

Then, two months later, when the position of General Manager of The Mall shopping complex—the country's then largest shopping complex—became vacant, she told me her decision to promote me to the position. After the initial euphoria, I had a couple of sleepless nights after finding out the turnover rate of General Managers since The Mall first opened in late 1987. In my worrisome mood, I turned to the *Art of War* and read:

> "His [the general] business is to assemble his troops and throw them into a critical position. He leads them deep into enemy territory to further his plans. He burns the boats and breaks the cooking pots ... if our penetration is deep and our soldiers know there is no turning back, they will concentrate their fighting spirit."

Thus, I found the solution: on the day my boss handed me the letter of promotion, to her surprise, I handed in my resignation. But I explained: "As you're a very demanding business-woman, I'm not sure if I could keep up with your rapid pace. Although I accept this promotion and would concentrate all my efforts to make The Mall the best shopping complex in the country, I still worry that my newness to this organization may have yet to earn your *full* trust and in lacking such necessary authority, I may somehow still fail you. When I do, just activate this letter which, as you may have noticed, is undated and I shall go."

Seeing my determination and seriousness to the extent of not even fearing to lose my job, she assured me of her total confidence and support. And true to her words, she very seldom interfered with my decisions while I was leading The Mall, which went on to win the much-coveted Tourist Development Corporation's Gold Award as the country's best shopping complex for two consecutive years thereafter.

Make yourself visible during meetings

The rationale behind the earlier two principles of having the courage to ask, speak up or take action, and impressing your boss of your sincerity is simply for you to be more visible. If you are not visible, there is a possibility that your boss may forget about you and may even ask: "How important is that person anyway?" So remember talent and hard work are still not enough. As they say, you have got to be seen to be smart.

An opportunity for you to be seen to be smart is during a meeting where influential people are present. Do not act as a mere observer lest they get the impression that you are a person who cannot contribute ideas or help in solving problems. Speak up even on issues which are not directly your area of concern to show you are a *total* company man.

WORKING WITH A BOSS BROUGHT IN FROM OUTSIDE

In addition to the earlier mentioned principles, try the following ones as well:

Get as close as possible to your boss

Part of your ability to succeed depends on cultivating mentors. The best way to do that is to feel comfortable with your boss because if you do not feel at ease with your boss, he may not feel comfortable with you either. I have met far too many people who try as much as possible to avoid their bosses because they feel uncomfortable of their bosses' temper or for some other reasons. Take this cue from Sun Tzu to heart:

"On intersecting ground, I will strengthen my alliances."

It is good strategy to ally yourself with your boss early, especially an incoming one. By maintaining close contact, you are making every effort to understand his expectations. Similarly, you are also helping your boss to understand you; otherwise, he will have difficulty in trusting you.

Don't make the mistake of comparing him with your previous boss

This is one sure way of turning your budding relationship with your new boss into an uncomfortable one, especially if you held your last boss in high esteem. Sun Tzu has this advice to offer:

"As water shapes its flow according to the ground, an army wins by relating to the enemy it faces. And just as water retains no constant shape, in war there shall be no constant condition."

Be open and accept your new boss with all his strengths and weaknesses. Thereafter, learn again from Sun Tzu, the following:

"A wise general considers both the advantages and disadvantages open to him. When considering the advantages, he makes his plans feasible; when considering the disadvantages, he finds ways to extricate himself from the difficulties."

When you try to appreciate your boss through observing his strengths and downplay his weaknesses, you may actually grow to like him. If not, try to put all personal feelings aside and see how you can still learn from him by emulating his strengths and avoiding his weaknesses. If you still cannot do that, then there is no help for you but to look for another boss to work for.

Be helpful to your boss

As a new manager in your organization, your boss will surely need all the help he can get. A primary area where an incoming manager will need help is information and a wise manager knows he should start learning from his immediate subordinates. As Sun Tzu observes:

> "Those who do not use local guides cannot benefit from the advantages of the ground."

Your boss will surely want to know who's who, how things are done, what has been going on in his own department, what's happening in others', etc. Useful information includes gossips about areas that are expanding or those about to be squeezed, which executives are feuding, and the status of different managers. So long as you are subtle in handing out such tidbits, you would have established your co-operation (sometimes even viewed as 'loyalty') with your boss because there has never been a boss who does not appreciate such information.

Another helping hand which you can extend to your boss is to supplement his deficiency. Everyone has weaknesses. I know an Executive Director who is weak in writing. Once when he asked one of his managers to write a speech (as a public figure, he was often invited to speak at company's and other functions) on his behalf, the manager worked very hard at it. As the Executive Director was impressed by the short and witty way he writes, the manager has since then been writing speeches and sometimes other correspondence on his behalf. Then when the recession struck and the company downsized, the Executive Director personally justified this manager's continued employment.

WORKING WITH BOSSES FROM
THE CONTROLLING COMPANY

Of the three situations, this is by far the most difficult to handle. It is rather sad that many bosses, especially those from large American corporations, are still ignorant of Sun Tzu's words:

> "Therefore, to win battles and make conquests and to take over all the subjects, but failing to rebuild or restore the welfare of what one gained would be a bad omen— it is considered as or so-called wasteful stay."

By not following these words, many bosses who are set on replacing the entire management team of companies they have taken over with their own people, have actually lost capable executives. Even if the entire management team is not replaced by those from the victorious corporation, a rash of corporate restructuring would usually follow a takeover.

Apart from advising those so affected to adopt a 'wait-and-see' attitude, I would further remind them to keep with the following Sun Tzu's sayings:

> "It is a principle of war that we do not assume the enemy will not come but instead we must be prepared for his coming; not to presume he will not attack but instead make our own positions unassailable."

By this, I mean you must always be prepared for the worst so that should it happen, you would have already taken steps to protect yourself. One way is to start looking for another job. In the event that you cannot find another job quick enough, then do as I did— incorporate my own company (you do not require much capital if you are offering services in terms of skills or expertise), have name cards printed with the title, 'Managing Director' (at least I can still hold my head high as an MD), and while using a registered address for mailing purposes, operate from my home's study room (fully air-conditioned and equipped with PC and fax machine) and when outside, in my car through handphone and pager.

Even if you are fortunate enough in that your new bosses have not yet served or do not seem to be in a hurry to serve you the 'walking' notice, you should still put into practice the following of Sun Tzu's advice:

> "Therefore, before the start of the battle, be as coy as a maiden; when your enemy lowers his guard and offers an opening, rush in like a hare out of its cage and the enemy will be unable to defend in time."

This means, quietly looking for another job and at the same time, carrying on applying those principles mentioned earlier on how to work with bosses in the hope that you may yet be accepted by the new management team from the 'victor' corporation.

WORKING WITH INDIRECT BOSSES

At some time or other, you may also be subject to scrutiny from other bosses who are not directly above you. That is why it is essential that you try as much as possible to cultivate the five virtues of a general and at the same time avoid the five dangerous faults as mentioned earlier in Chapter 4 so that at all times you can still project a favorable image to these senior executives.

There was an occasion in my career-life when I was trying very hard to rise in ranks but found myself making no headway. I activated my network ("Form alliances with neighboring States on intersecting ground") and did some checking ("If you know yourself and know your enemy, in a hundred battles you will never fear the result") to learn that a certain senior executive was opposing my promotion.

Although the discovery was quite upsetting, instead of succumbing to demoralization (such is only for losers), I tried to do something constructive: find out why—his resistance may have a basis in fact, e.g. I may have some negative behaviors or he has some perceptions of my performance which may be unfounded, or simply out of wrong 'chemistry', that is, he just does not like me.

I thanked God it was not the latter. From my sources, I learned that he heard somewhere from someone that I possessed an impetuous nature which resulted in my mishandling an assignment once. Even though that was a minor assignment which happened almost two years previously, and I had by then already learned from the unpleasant experience, were not in his consideration at all. He was simply prejudiced and I know that while I would not be able to turn him overnight into an avid supporter, or even a lukewarm one, I should still have to do something to change the negative impression so that at least his misguided view of my potential can be reduced enough to allow other friendly and unbiased parties to push through their support for me. I drew much comfort and inspiration from Sun Tzu's words:

> "A wise general considers both the advantages and disadvantages opened to him. When considering the advantages, he makes his plan feasible; when considering the disadvantages, he finds way to extricate himself from the difficulties."

Thereafter, I treaded most carefully whenever he was present. In meetings where we both sat, I deliberately 'reined in my horses' and refrained from coming up with immediate replies. I chose my answers carefully after putting on a show of analytical thoughtfulness. Two months later, I learned he did not oppose me anymore.

And never align yourself so closely to your immediate boss that you have no time for, or worse, snub the other key senior executives in your company. I know one executive who hitched his wagon too closely to his boss that when the latter died in an air crash, he was left in a lurch. The 'hawks' from the parent company soon moved in to carve out their own empires and as he did not have any friends and allies, he found it so unbearable that he did not stay long thereafter.

WORKING WITH BAD BOSSES

Bosses come in all shapes and sizes. Some got their high positions on account of their experience and (or) qualifications. A few are said to have got their plum jobs by 'outliving' all other potential candidates. Quite a number have been known to have acquired top jobs as a result of 'connections' and 'strings-pulling'. In some countries where corruption is rampant, there have also been stories of people 'buying' their way into top jobs, especially in the public sector. Then there are those who 'talked' their way into high positions. Regardless of how they got their jobs or how capable they are at their jobs, there are good bosses and bad ones co-existing with one another.

The bad ones, however, appear to outnumber the good. Associated Press reported in June 1995 that when a certain Mr Jim Miller mounted a search in the United States for nominations of bosses in two categories—the best and the worst—receipts of the latter outpaced the former. But while Mr Miller has defined bad bosses as those who are cheap, foul-mouthed, heartless, and nasty, I would rather see bad bosses as those who are cowardly, dishonest, incompetent, interfering, uncommunicative or unreasonable. In other words, they may be bad but not necessarily wicked (there is no way one can work with a wicked person). Even then, the badness can come in varying degrees—from a mild dosage to a lethal one. Let us look at Sun Tzu's classification of bosses (or 'rulers' as he would call them) and turn to his war principles on how to deal with bad bosses.

THE THREE TYPES OF BAD BOSSES

According to Sun Tzu, there are three ways whereby a ruler can bring misfortune upon his army.

The Ignorant Boss

The first way whereby a ruler could bring misfortune upon his army would be:

> "By commanding an army to advance or retreat, when ignorant on whether to advance or retreat. This is called, 'hobbling the army'."

A bad boss usually became that way out of insecurity. One of the roots of insecurity is a lack of knowledge. And a strange phenomenon of life is that the more one does not know, the more one feels the urge to prove he knows. As a result, wrong decisions tend to be made. If you do not want to be ordered around blindly by an ignorant boss, then influence his decision-making. Know your boss's insecurity in advance so that you not only avoid jittering him but will know what essential information he needs so that you can subtly provide him with such information before any decision is taken. In the event that your boss has already decided, and you feel it is a bad decision, try to apply this advice given by Sun Tzu:

> "Subtle and secretive, the skilled learns to be invisible and silent to control the enemy's fate."

Remember Gandhi's strategy of passive resistance resulting in India's eventual independence. That is being subtle, secretive, invisible and silent. Then, there was this article I once read which tells how the great Dave Packard himself took an on-the-spot decision that all work should cease on an electronic device under development at Hewlett-Packard. He said: "When I come round in a year's time, I don't want to see the product in the lab." His engineers cunningly ignored his order to cease work by sticking to the letter of the great decision-maker's words—they worked relentlessly to finish the product within a year, to Hewlett-Packard's considerable profit. Again, we find the ingredients of subtlety, secretiveness, invisibility and silence as Sun Tzu has prescribed.

Or how about:

> "When I wish to avoid a fight, I can prevent an
> engagement even though the battlelines had been drawn
> by diverting my enemy with something odd and
> unexpected thrown his way."

The something odd and unexpected could work like this: when a really pushy Director of Marketing started breathing hard down the neck of his Manager, the latter recalled a recent chance meeting with an old classmate who has since became chief of a prestigious "head-hunting" firm. The friend had asked for recommendation of possible candidates for the position of marketing vice-president of a *Fortune-500* firm expanding into the Asia-Pacific region. The Manager recommended his boss and within two months, his boss left to join the new firm.

The Rigid (Inflexible) Boss
The second way of bringing misfortune to an army would be:

> "By trying to administer an army the same way he
> administers a kingdom, when ignorant of military
> affairs. This causes the officers to be perplexed."

While ignorance is again the root of this behavior, this type of boss usually tends to be obstinate. You can almost say his ignorance is by choice. Such bosses can see no other viewpoints but their own.

Shortly after a Manager took up his appointment to head the subsidiary of a multinational company in his country, he found the office's computers were loaded with pirated softwares. When a journalist friend tipped him off that certain software corporations were out to nab legitimate corporations with illegitimate softwares, he knew he has got to do something fast or risk getting caught and fined heavily. He immediately reviewed the office's software needs, ordered the purchase of legitimate softwares to replace the pirated ones which he immediately erased from the computers' hard-disks.

Believing he had saved the company from out-of-court settlement fee running into a couple of hundred thousand dollars had his firm been caught, he was thus surprised to hear that the CEO at the regional office was upset by his actions. He found out later from his Regional Manager that the CEO, who was irked after being told by the Finance Director (a stickler for procedures) that procedures were not followed (that is, a proposal must be submitted and approval obtained for any capital expenditure), and wanted the softwares returned to the vendor.

His immediate reaction was: "Heck! Doesn't Mr Horse know the basic principles of offer and acceptance in the Law of Contract? Besides, how are we going to work without softwares? And you mean to say, he would rather we take a chance with the authorities and should we get caught, he's prepared for an out-of-court settlement fee which could come to a hundred times more than the cost of the software? Talk of 'cutting one's nose to spite the face'."

Then, the Manager recalled Sun Tzu's advice:

"To be successful in warfare, we must pretend we are keeping to the enemy's designs.

He formatted and put up a Capital Expenditure Form for the software purchase and faxed off to the Finance Director, together with a memo which reads:

"Hi Jock,
Talk of 'putting the cart before the horse', we have done it this time.

The breach in procedure was however unintended and inevitable considering (i) the situation here was quite critical (I had a telephone alert from a former journalist colleague); (ii) the absence of written guidelines (we did not even have a Capital Expenditure Form); and (iii) my personal belief that talking to my Regional Manager was good enough.

Well, we are learning—and in the absence of a Capital Expenditure Form, I have even drafted one up for submission of this case ... and future ones, if you think this format is in order.

My regrets for all the 'bzzzzzing'."

The next day, he personally telephoned the Finance Director who said the Form had been approved and will be faxed back the same day. The Regional Manager who has all along appreciated his effort, also tipped him off that the CEO was no longer upset since the Finance Director had been appeased.

The Autocratic Boss
The third way of bringing misfortune to an army would be:

"By using the army officers without discretion, when ignorant of the military principles of being flexible with

cumstances. This causes doubts in the minds of
officers."

Here, a combination of ignorance and inflexibility could only mean an autocratic boss. Such bosses simply wants to do things his way. To handle this kind of bosses, again, let us recall the following of Sun Tzu's sayings:

"As water shapes its flow according to the ground, an army wins by relating to the enemy it faces. And just as water retains no constant shape, in war there will be no constant condition."

Be like water— use cleverness against his ignorance and be flexible against his inflexibility. Cleverness means being well-informed and with information at your fingertips, you are able to prepare your boss for your proposal which must never be sprung on him as a surprise. This means you must build up his awareness through dialogue and personal contact well ahead of the proposal. The point here is never give an autocratic boss a chance to come to any decision without your having first influencing him because once an autocratic boss has made a commitment, it is almost impossible to get him to change his mind.

THE REALITY OF BAD BOSSES

I sometimes question the reality of bad bosses. By this, I mean are we really in the position to judge a boss as bad? Or could bad bosses exist merely because, in believing ourselves to be the victims, we thus perceive them to be so? As Sun Tzu says:

"The supreme skill in commanding troops is in the shapeless command. Then, the prying of the subtlest spies cannot penetrate for the laying of plans against you. The shapes I take shall lay plans for victory but

72

such are beyond the comprehension of the masses. While all can see the external aspects, none can understand the way I scored my victory."

and

"It is the business of a general to be calm and mysterious; fair and composed. He must be capable of mystifying his officers and men so that they are ignorant of his true intentions."

and again,

"Assign tasks to your soldiers without detailing your plan."

So who are we to judge our bosses and say they are wrong in doing what they are doing or have done? Is it right for us to judge them solely from our perceptions?

Take Akio Morita, for instance. When he decided to go ahead to manufacture a miniaturized, portable, personal hi-fi, nearly everybody else at Sony Corp objected to the proposal but the Walkman turned out to be one of Sony's greatest money-spinning innovations in the mass market. Before the money started to roll in, surely there must be those who had condemned him as a fool. At a micro level, when your boss refused to grant you leave for three days to take your family for a jaunt in the countryside because he is short-handed, are you going to condemn him as a bad boss? As I have told a few of my managers previously, as professional managers, we do not exist for the sake of being popular. We have a job to do. Be firm if we have to, but be fair about it. Sun Tzu could sum it up most appropriately:

"If a general is too indulgent; if he loves his men too
much to enforce his commands, and cannot assert
control when troops are in disorder, then the soldiers
are similar to spoilt children and are useless."

True, there are bad bosses in existence but perhaps the find-
ings by Mr Jim Miller that bad ones outnumber the good, as mentioned earlier, could be wrong. The large numbers could in part
be the result of our narrow and prejudiced perceptions.

I too have personally suffered perceptions. On numerous occasions, tea-ladies had told me something to this effect: "Mr
Khoo, you are blessed with such a good life. You get a high pay
and only come to office to spend the entire morning either talking on the telephone or drinking tea and reading newspapers,
then off you go for lunch, and after lunch, back to write some reports for a couple of hours before going home. I hope my children will have such a blessed life when they grow up." Would
these tea-ladies (and some other staff who thought the same but
did not voice out) not think of me as being undeserving of the
high remuneration given I contributed so little? Ah, perceptions
... perceptions, this is what makes one's life so interesting and so
complicating.

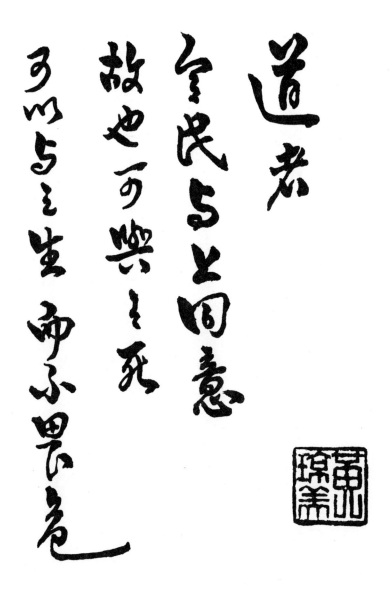

道者令民与上同意故也可與之死可以与之生而不畏危

"By moral law, I mean that which causes the people to be in total accord with their ruler, so that they will follow him in life and unto death without fear for their lives and undaunted by any peril."

6

WORKING WITH SUBORDINATES

NO MANAGER MUST ever ignore the level of support of his subordinates. A manager's power is really inherent in the subordinates whom he can influence to do things the way he wants. Without such influence or support, big titles really mean nothing at all.

THE POWER OF EMPOWERMENT

It is quite surprising that quite a number of managers do not see the power which can come from empowering their subordinates. If you realize that your subordinates also need to have some power themselves in order to get things done and you empower them accordingly, results will then be achievable. By empowerment, I mean allowing your subordinates to use whatever power they have to do their jobs *their* way. While you should still watch over them to see that they do not get into serious trouble, give them room to decide and learn from their mistakes with some advice from you to set them right again.

A friend of mine joined a local retailing company as General Manager and enthusiastically went about his job. As his boss had circulated a memo citing his authority limit to approve capital expenditure up to $2,000, he once gave his approval to buy a computer costing $1,950 to facilitate tracking of customers' orders. Two days later, his boss's secretary told the Management Information Manager to cancel the order with the vendor because the boss had taken upon himself not to approve the purchase. The General Manager then realized his boss is a pompous and self-important man who is always diminishing his managers in his grasp for power. It has been some 2,500 years since Sun Tzu last wrote:

"Put your men in positions where there is no escape and even when facing death, they will not run ... Thus, without the need of supervision, they will be alert, and without being asked, they will support their general; without being ordered, they will trust him."

The onus is therefore on you to create such situations for victory and depriving your subordinates of power is certainly not good management. Such is an act of insecurity or incompetence on the part of a manager.

This is what Paul Chan, the former General Manager and Director for Computer Systems Organization (South Asia) of Hewlett-Packard Singapore (Sales) Pte. Ltd., once told me: "My power actually comes from my people's strengths. That's why I like to empower them because by giving them responsibility and helping them to develop as I develop, they are motivated to stay and I get better people who contribute to our organization." It was after $17^{1}/_{2}$ successful years with HP that Paul left to become Managing Director and Vice-President (Asean) of Compaq Asia Pte. Ltd.

It was reported recently that Hewlett-Packard received the Distinguished Partner in Progress Award from the Singapore Government on its 25th anniversary in the island-republic. Further probing by a journalist found that despite high labor mobility, 47 of its original 62 employees are still with the company all these years. When asked to elaborate, HP's Director of Human Resource (Southeast Asia), Soo Kok Leng, said: "Tell employees what needs to be done, but do not tell them how to do it. Reward them when they do well, and help them readjust when the work situation changes." This has resulted in creating a work environment that makes employees want to stay on.

WAYS OF EMPOWERING SUBORDINATES

There are many ways you can empower your subordinates:

Earn their respect and gain their acceptance

Before you can try out the many ways of empowerment, you must first apply this one—earn their respect and gain their acceptance otherwise whatever you say or do may be regarded as a joke. Even Sun Tzu realizes this fact:

> "Secure the loyalty of your troops first before
> disciplining them or they will not be submissive."

Sometimes your men may even put you to test, especially if you are new to the organization. When I first became Sales & Marketing Manager for Malayan Sugar Manufacturing Company Berhad in Kuala Lumpur, Malaysia, a couple of my Sales Executives who were older and experienced in their fields, tried to bait me by referring their favorite problems— demanding (for price advantage) or plain nasty wholesalers—to me and see how I handled them. I remembered what Sun Tzu said:

> "He [the general] leads the army into battle just like a
> person who has climbed to the heights and then kicks
> away the ladder behind him so as to put them in a
> desperate situation."

In their positions, they had expected me to either back away or play safe in avoiding the issue. Instead, after getting them to brief me on the particular problem on hand, I would usually ask them to accompany me to meet the wholesaler concerned. And the result usually turned out like what Sun Tzu has observed:

> "The people of Wu and Yueh mutually hate each other
> but when they sail in the same boat tossed by the wind,

they will help each other just like the right hand
co-operates with the left."

Being in the same boat and facing a common problem, we
would naturally have to support each other and try to solve it.

Instil pride in themselves

In Chapter 1 of the *Art of War*, Sun Tzu elaborates on the 'Moral
Law':

> "By Moral Law, I mean that which causes the people to
> be in total accord with their ruler, so that they will
> follow him in life and unto death without fear for their
> lives and undaunted by any peril."

Thus, shortly after assuming my position as Country Manager and Director of Adia Personnel Services Pte. Ltd. in Singapore, I asked my staff who would be the most important person
in the company. Naturally, they pointed at me since I have been
assigned the task of turning the company around.

I then drew an organizational chart (see page 81) made up of
concentric circles instead of the usual pyramidal hierarchy. When
each one of them was handed a copy of the chart during a meeting, I explained: "You're right, I'm important because I am the
brain who is going to strategize our turnaround. But brains are all
quite vulnerable if unprotected. That's why I have a Business Development Manager on my left and a Finance and Administration Manager on my right. But out there at the 'battlefront'
where the 'fighting' is, I have my Consultants to fulfill clients'
staffing needs, my Administrative Assistants to provide support
services and follow up on invoices, and my Receptionist to re-
ceive visitors and ensure calls are taken. If my front-line troops
and my left and right hands are not vigilant, and allow any of my

enemy to get through, then I'll be in trouble!" That showed them that they were important as well.

Organization Chart of
Adia Personnel Services Pte. Ltd.

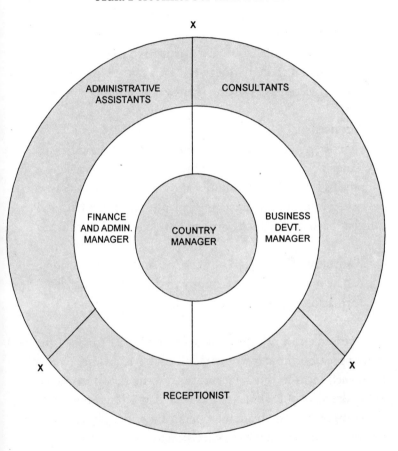

Date: December 1, 1995.

Supposing I had done the traditional pyramidal chart, would you think any of my Consultants, Administrative Assistants, or my Receptionist would feel proud being right there at the bottom without 'command'?

True enough, the organization chart of mine was a political move designed at motivating my people. But since I carried out the entire exercise with sincerity (remember, this is one of the virtues which Sun Tzu encouraged a general to have?), the positiveness cannot be disputed. Once your staff can feel proud of themselves (and of you), they are on their way to empowerment.

Gain consensus

The next step in empowering people would be the introduction of change or decision-making which are based on consensus. By consensus, I do not mean blindly allowing everyone to say whatever they like and (or) do as they please. Rather, what I have in mind is 'harmony' which Sun Tzu has elaborated as follows:

> "Without harmony in the State, no military expedition can be made; without harmony in the army, no battle formation can be directed."

I would either ask for ideas or I would share my idea and ask what my subordinates would think of it. Most times, we would try to sell ideas to one another, with some modifications made along the way but whatever has been decided upon would have the consensus of my team members. Sometimes, if time does not permit, I would then take the decision myself even if such were to make me unpopular. After all, do not forget what I have shared with you in the last chapter—as professional managers, we exist not for the sake of being popular but rather to get our job done. It is sad that many managers in their eagerness to be accepted by their subordinates become fearful of hostility and refuse to confront and correct their subordinates, thus end up becoming ineffective in a world of conflicting goals and interests.

Give rewards and incentives freely

At time of writing this chapter, one of my Consultants had cheerfully worked beyond office hours in the past few days to fulfill an urgent executive search order, two other consultants have been consistently contributing to productivity which are measurable and an Administrative Assistant have been diligently 'chasing' outstanding debtors. While the outstanding ones received letters of commendation, recognizing their contributions, all received double cinema passes for a weekend. It did not cost much but as one Consultant told me: "It's very motivating to be appreciated." It may be 506BC then but Sun Tzu has already noted:

> "In battle, those who capture more than ten chariots
> from the enemy should be rewarded."

and

> "When plundering the countryside and having captured
> new lands, divide the profits among your men."

Do not just reward your people but also empower them to give rewards and incentives. So often I have heard complaints by those in the lower hierarchy that they have to abide strictly by the rules and have no power to use their judgement or make decisions. This could especially be disastrous in a service organization. For this reason, while I was Director of Operations with Kentucky Fried Chicken in Singapore, I was always delighted when Restaurant Managers gave their crew members the power to offer free drinks to customers who were kept waiting for their food due to our own operational faults, e.g. out-of-product situation, short of staff, etc. Sun Tzu would have approved too, having said:

> "Bestow rewards without regard to customary rules,
> issue orders without regard to prescribed procedures."

While such practices have a good effect on the customers, I have noticed an even bigger effect on the staff because it made them feel great that the management trusted them.

Be consistent in giving instructions

Nothing is more infuriating or frustrating than inconsistency in instructions. I once worked for a boss who told me I should entertain in order to bring in business opportunities. Then, when I brought a few business associates to lunch at the company-owned restaurants, I was told I should not be too extravagant (even though each of the five meal tickets averages less than $100). He also wanted me to visit clients but later complained I was too often out of the office. Take these words of Sun Tzu for example:

> "If the commands used in leading troops are consistent,
> soldiers will be disciplined. If not, soldiers are inclined to
> be disobedient. If a general's commands are consistently
> credible and obeyed, he enjoys good relationship with
> his men."

To instil consistency into your commands, it is essential that your team members are clear about your goals and your success criteria. Since your team may be working with different parties—external customers, staff of other departments, other senior managers, etc.— conflicting demands may abound and you, as the team leader, must be able to identify the key people involved so as to negotiate success criteria with them, and thereafter communicate such negotiations with your team who may then understand and accept responsibility for their roles.

Invest in training and development programs

It is pointless to empower your subordinates who may still be unable to do their jobs for want of skills or knowledge. It is thus surprising that for his era, Sun Tzu could yet be so far more advanced than some contemporary bosses who would refrain from investing in their employees' training and development, since the great strategist has been known to say:

> "Nourish your soldiers and build up their internal strengths so that they are free of hundreds of diseases, and this will ensure victory."

Nourishment can be more than just feeding one's stomach. You can also feed one's mind which is what training and development are all about so that empowered employees can actually go about their jobs with confidence and skill.

Select personnel without fear or favor

Astute managers know their power is enhanced by having capable people around them. So, apart from using their power in a way which attracts such people rather than inhibiting or repelling them, learn also the need to select personnel without fear or favor. Sun Tzu has made the following observation:

> "A skilled commander conserves energy from the situation instead of wasting his men. He selects his men according to their talents and uses them to exploit the situation."

It thus came as no surprise to me that after I completed my studies in Scotland and came to Singapore in August 1991, I was jobless for nearly four months. After having attained the high position of General Manager in my last job and further graduated with an MBA (with distinction), I found many senior executives lacking the courage to take me on, even for a departmental head position. Could they perhaps view me as a potential threat who may eventually compete for their jobs? And after working in Singapore the past few years, I also discovered that the mindset of most local employers tends to be confined to two boxes. The first is the 'box of industry' where unless you have worked in a particular industry, you will not be considered a likely candidate. The next one is the 'box of function' where in the absence of working experience and knowledge of a particular job function, say, Finance, your likelihood of being selected for a position in that function will be most slim. Do not be like these narrow-minded employers but be more open in selecting capable people to work for you.

DISADVANTAGES OF EMPOWERMENT

While the advantages of empowerment outweigh the disadvantages, it is still to our benefit to be aware of the latter in order to handle them as they come.

Unnecessary delays from seeking consensus
It is no wonder that Sun Tzu observes:

> "Victory is the main object in war. If this is long
> delayed, weapons will become blunt and the ardor of
> the soldiers will be dampened."

and

> "Thus, while we have heard of stupid haste in war, we
> have not yet seen a clever operation that was prolonged.

History has shown that there has never been a country benefiting from prolonged warfare."

That is why many clever and strong bosses, while seeking consensus to preserve the internal harmony, could yet be most decisive when it comes to getting the job done.

When empowerment runs counter to the corporate culture

In some more traditional organizations whose culture tends to be more restrictive or centralized, when you empower your subordinates, your delegation of power may actually threaten your colleagues and (or) even bosses. They may fear that you will lose control, or worse, may feel challenged by your excellent results. If their subordinates, especially their best people, show any inclination to join you (or even praise you), you could end up without sponsorship of peers and bosses. That is why in Chapter 3, I have advised that one should be careful in choosing the right organization with the right culture to start with. If not, then perhaps the following advice from Sun Tzu may still be helpful:

"What the ancients called a skilful fighter is one who not only wins but wins with ease. But the victories will neither earn him a reputation for wisdom nor credit for valor. For victories are such, they are gained in circumstances that have not been revealed and he thus wins no reputation for wisdom; and as the enemy submits without bloodshed, he receives no credit for valor."

Sometimes it pays to go about your work quietly but steadily. To do this, you must see yourself as what Sun Tzu has described as 'a general who is the precious jewel of his State':

"Thus, the general who advances without coveting fame and withdraws without fearing disgrace, but whose sole intention is to protect the people and serve his ruler, is the precious jewel of the State."

This means whatever you do, you are doing with the company's interest at heart and not your own. When your peers and bosses see you in this light and trust your sincerity, they would not only stop feeling threatened but may even emulate your action.

When empowered staff become too powerful

A friend of mine who was an Accounts Director with an advertising agency told me this story: "When we adopted a growth strategy, we decided to create another level of management under my charge. Accordingly, I promoted some of my executives as well as some who were recommended from the other groups. Thereafter, I relinquished some of my power and controls to them. Six months later, I found myself out in the cold when these 'young Turks' took over all client liaison and most of these clients had actually lost contact with me."

My friend had only himself to blame because he has failed to heed one of Sun Tzu's very wise observations:

"When the common soldiers are stronger than their officers, they will insubordinate. When the officers are too strong and the troops are weak, the result is collapse."

As I have mentioned earlier, it is important to train and develop your subordinates so that they can perform what they have been empowered to perform. But as their leader, you must still see to your own personal development so that you are still at least one step ahead to ensure control.

凡

用兵之法
將受命於君
合軍聚眾
交和而舍

"Without harmony in the State, no military expedition can be made; without harmony in the army, no battle formation can be directed."

7

WORKING WITH PEERS

WHEREVER YOU WORK, whether the hierarchy is large or small, in whatever industry, you are bound to have competitors eyeing the same places in the sun that you have set your sights on. These people are mostly your peers. As their power often equals yours, if not surpassing yours, it is necessary to learn how to work with them.

THE SINCERITY APPROACH

In advocating positive politics, I have always been emphasizing on the sincerity approach. If you could recall, this is one of the five virtues which Sun Tzu encouraged a general to cultivate. It is my personal belief (having learned from experience) that good begets good, thus sincerity begets sincerity. But do not confuse sincerity with being naive or gullible. You will be most naive and gullible if you see everyone as a saint and thereafter let your guard down indiscriminately.

Even a saint is not perfect. By sincerity, I am actually referring to your basic willingness to ensure internal harmony through working closely with others and respecting their rights and needs.

INTERNAL HARMONY

The principle behind the sincerity approach is motivated by Sun Tzu who pointed out:

"Without harmony in the State, no military expedition can be made; without harmony in the army, no battle formation can be directed."

He further warns:

"Those skilful commanders of old knew how to split the enemy's unity between the front and rear troops; to prevent co-operation between the main force and the reinforcement; to hinder the stronger troops from rescuing the weaker ones, and subordinates from supporting their superiors."

Far too many stories have already been told of organizations which have been considerably weakened—if not wrecked—as a result of intensive in-fighting amongst the executives. Sometimes the competitors may have given a helping hand in igniting off such in-fighting.

THE REALITY OF CO-EXISTENCE

But even when people recognize the importance of working together, the nature of any given job often combines contradictory elements such as personality differences that create various kinds of role conflict. Anything to do with personality is highly relative and subjective. No one can be that perfect as being capable at dealing with everyone or comfortable in every situation. Besides, what is in the interest of one manager may not be in the interest of another, and even when their goals are similar, their approaches and motivation may differ.

A manager who is rapidly scaling the corporate ladder may not worry as much about the competition, unlike those who climb more slowly, simply because he is getting what he wants from the company. But for those who cannot get what they want—in terms of advancement and security—they may find themselves caught between the requirements of their business lives on one hand, and the requirements of their emotional lives on the other. So although this morning's meeting (as with all meetings) is over, and in your opinion, has gone smoothly enough, what were the people in the room really thinking about each other?

What I am trying to say is that the very same environment which requires a great deal of untroubled personal interaction also demands a great deal of competition. As executives, it is expected of us to compete not only on behalf of our companies but also to compete within, for power and position, i.e. against our colleagues.

This is why in Chapter 2 earlier, I urged you to go for power albeit in a positive way. Once you have decided to work in a corporation, there is no escape. If you are adverse to power, then my advice is to stay home and learn to cook, sew and wash. Even at home, as with some large traditional families where the in-laws live together, politicking may yet be rife.

FAIR COMPETITION

Once you could bring yourself to understand this tension between teamwork and career competition, which could at times lead to some emotional stress, you could then become more tolerant and seek to compete as fairly as possible. As Sun Tzu rationalizes:

> "One who does not thoroughly understand the calamity
> of war shall be unable to thoroughly comprehend the
> advantages of war."

While competition can offer benefits for the winner, it can also bear terrible consequences for the loser. It is thus in the interest of all concerned to compete fairly for the so-called 'win-win' situation. There are many ways of competing fairly. But first, let us see what Sun Tzu has to say:

> "Fighting to win one hundred victories in one battle is not the supreme skill. To break the enemy's resistance without fighting is the supreme skill."

This, then appears to be the essence of fair competition which could take the following forms:

Impress your colleagues of your sincerity

This is just a repetition of what I have said earlier when touching on the sincerity approach which goes to emphasize its importance. But being sincere is really not good enough. You have got to demonstrate your sincerity. According to Sun Tzu:

> "Thus, the general skilled in war places priority in attacking the enemy's strategy."

Here, I would regard "attacking the enemy's strategy" as merely setting right whatever misperception which my colleagues may have of me or whatever I am trying to do.

Many times in the past when I came up with proposals to change the way things were done, I would first sought out my colleagues before submitting the proposals to my boss. I have realized very early in my career that what is good for me may sometimes be bad for others. For example, a Human Resource Manager's generous compensation scheme may certainly attract, motivate and retain employees (he may even become a hero in the process), but the same scheme may turn out to be the Financial Controller's nightmare as he has to ensure there are adequate funds flow to finance the scheme. By first bringing my proposals to my colleagues, I would have accomplished two things: (i) demonstrated my sincere objectivity; and (ii) allow them to share their views. This will pave the way for us to work closely together towards an essential compromise if required.

You can also impress your colleagues of your sincerity by not encroaching into his territory. Sun Tzu says:

"After leaving your own country, march your army across the border and you are in frontier ground. Where there are convergences of all roads from different directions, that is known as open ground ... on frontier ground, I will make sure that our troops are well linked-up ... on open ground, I will increase our vigilance."

I interpret this to mean one must tread carefully when going into another executive's 'territory', e.g. his room, department, or part of the building, etc. Even if it is on official business, it is prudent to give him a call in advance and let him know when you are going over to his area, whom you would like to see, and share with him the reason for being there. If you are unable to call in advance, then drop by his office first to put him into the picture. If you think this is silly, then ask yourself honestly how you will feel if your colleague from any department or division come into your work area and without calling on you, sit down and start working with one of your staff. By observing this protocol, you could be saving yourself a lot of unnecessary 'battles' and embarrassment arising from territorial confrontations.

Form alliances

In Sun Tzu's time, military warfare can sometimes be averted by making sure your enemies do not gang up against you. This was what the great strategist said:

"The next best is to disrupt any alliances of the enemy."

This saying, however, should not be applied blindly to the way you work with your peers. Read it instead to understand the significance which Sun Tzu has given to alliance— never allowing enemies to gang up on you but seeking to ally yourself with friendly forces. As he has advised in a later part of the *Art of War*:

> "Form alliances with neighboring States on intersecting ground."

I have personally found from experience that the higher one climbs, the more one shall need allies. This is because mistakes made at the top level usually tend to be more critical and obvious. And without powerful friends to back you up, one of those mistakes could easily spell the end of your career one day. In this respect, one must always work at keeping one's alliances alive. Instead of using one's network for short-term gains, the astute manager builds up a series of long-term alliances. This means that he will still stay in touch with people even though there may be no favor to ask.

Develop assertive behavior
To continue with Sun Tzu's advice from the previous:

> "... to be followed by the confrontation of the enemy's army."

I would interpret 'confrontation' to mean assertiveness which is to stand up for your rights and needs. In doing so, you actually risk confrontation with other people. When one states an opinion, it is inevitable that there may yet be others who would disagree with him. However, if you are skilful in going about your assertive behavior, the risk of confronting people and rubbing them the wrong way could actually be reduced. Such skills can be learned and practised to perfection. In 1983 when I became Sales & Marketing Manager for Malayan Sugar Manufacturing Company Berhad, I learned that assertiveness worked best with my colleagues when I adopted the following steps:

1. be informative, i.e. put my colleagues in the picture;
2. say what I want, i.e. be as clear as I can and not beat about the bush unnecessarily;
3. show them the benefits; and
4. also tell them the likely problems.

Leave an 'escape route' for your opponent

Sun Tzu continues to counsel:

> "The worst policy of all is to attack walled cities. Attack walled cities only as a last resort."

I would consider a 'walled city' as a situation where the confrontation has reached a 'deadlock' with either party being unable to back off gracefully. But again, if you are skilled in your assertiveness, such a situation can be easily resolved by taking the following advice from Sun Tzu:

> "When surrounding an enemy, leave him an escape route. Do not press an enemy to desperation. This is the way of maneuvering an army."

Standing up for your rights and needs does not mean ignoring the rights and needs of others. By respecting the rights and needs of others, they will in turn respect yours. In this way, if you are ever caught in a confrontation with a peer, leave him an 'escape route', that is, a way to consent without having to climb down in a humiliating way.

An 'escape route' story which I enjoyed tremendously was that of an elderly Japanese patriarch who, as President of a family-owned pharmaceutical company, was caught in an embarrassing situation one day when during a meeting, his son spoke up emotionally against his policy. In a culture where no junior executive, let alone one's offspring, would dare speak against the patriarch boss, such a confrontation could be considered extremely impolite. It could even be considered shameful since both father and son were involved and everyone present expected the patriarch boss to try regain his dignity by firing his son which again, would be a major blow to both corporate and family relationships. When no reaction came from the President, all the executives turned towards him with averted looks and abated breaths, and to their surprise and relief, found the old man snoring gently with his eyes closed. Since the patriarch boss was asleep and did not hear his son's outburst, he was not shamed and thus need not have to take any action against his son. The son, who had by then realized his mistake in being overly emotional, also felt grateful for that reprieve. The person who told me that story confided to me at the ending that the old man was actually conscious but merely pretended to have had dozed off so as to avail himself and his son the essential 'escape routes'.

Watch against anger whatever the provocation
In any 'deadlocked' situation, do not allow your temper to get the better of you. As Sun Tzu continues to advise:

> "If the general cannot control his anger and sends his soldiers to swarm up the walls like ants, then one-third of his troops will be killed without capturing the city."

As I have mentioned earlier in Chapter 4, when there is hostility and anger around, the one who could stay calm and in control, is the one who actually wields power. This is mainly due to an unwritten code of business that executives must keep their emotions under control lest work become more charged and rela-

tionships less stable. As one CEO told me: "The pretense of colle-
giality and unselfish team play must be maintained at all costs. As
an executive, to act out one's frustrations and mistrust is unpro-
fessional and thus, unforgivable. But surely you know ... even
Sun Tzu has said something about this." I believe he was referring
to Sun Tzu's suggestion that:

> "All warfare is based on deception. Therefore, when
> capable, pretend to be incapable; when active, inactive;
> when near, make the enemy believe that you are far
> away; when far away, that you are near ... If he is prone
> to choleric temper, irritate him."

From this, we can see all the more, the need to remain calm so
as not to be easily provoked to lose your cool, your credibility,
and perhaps your career.

And don't ever threaten

Threats almost never work because your peers, as I have said earlier, could be as powerful as you are, if not more powerful. Besides, threats are a reflection of one's immaturity. Even Sun Tzu
has found that:

> "When the enemy's envoy speaks humbly but he is
> secretly preparing his force, he will advance. But when
> the language is fierce and the enemy threatens to attack,
> he is looking for a way to retreat."

Indeed, I am more wary of a person who speaks humbly and
softly than one who blusters and threatens. If you threaten people into entrenched positions, the chances of their fighting back
are high. And if you threaten powerful people, they will have no
choice but to hit back or risk losing face. And later even if they
wish to, they will be unable to back off with the result that it is
you who lose.

INDIRECT PEERS

This chapter will be incomplete if I neglect to talk about indirect peers, or those colleagues we do not get to see everyday. These people are usually those who are located in different offices or come visiting only once in a while from the regional or head office. Compared with those colleagues we deal with everyday, working with such indirect peers tends to be much more difficult because your irregular contact with them means you may not be able to develop an easy and predictable way of interaction as you could with those you meet daily. This could be what Sun Tzu has in mind when he first wrote:

> "If we cannot fathom the designs of our neighboring
> States, we cannot enter into alliances in advance."

All of this mean that we just have to work harder to present, explain and expound in lengthy and often discomforting details. As I have found out from experience, anyone who do not develop the skills and patience to do this will undoubtedly suffer frustrating and irritating experiences with such indirect colleagues.

Once, when concentrating my efforts to improve my firm's business, I neglected visiting managers from the regional office. Thus, although our independently-commissioned survey subsequently showed an improvement in our business positioning, my boss told me the regional President had some doubts about me. I learned that he had heard I was running around building a 'Sun Tzu's cult' amongst my managers. And despite improvement in sales and profitability at the end of the year, it still did not help change the regional President's perception of me. So you see, I too have made stupid mistakes despite my knowledge of the *Art of War*.

故明君賢將所以動而勝人成功出於眾者先知也

"The enlightened ruler and the wise general can subdue the
enemy whenever they move and they can achieve
superhuman feats because they have foreknowledge."

8

THE POWER OF INFORMATION

TO SURVIVE IN 'enemy territory', so to speak, more employees than ever have begun to realize that the key to success is information. 'Enemy territory' is not just the marketplace out there but in this case, could refer to the internal workplace where there is a daily need for executives to know what is going on around them, to stay fine-tuned to the changing alliances and subtle power shifts.

SPY VS SPY

According to Dee Soder, the CEO of Endymion Co., a New York-based executive-advisory firm that counsels professionals on how to navigate tricky professional waters, one way to effectively hone our survival instinct in corporate life is to make-believe we are spies and our office is in a foreign country. The 'spying' would mostly consist of watching out for unusual behavior, such as when one executive spends time talking to someone whom he does not usually talk to. This helps one to anticipate changes and pave the way for one's own advancement. This is in keeping with one of Sun Tzu's most often quoted sayings:

"If you know yourself and know your enemy, in a hundred battles you will never fear the result. When you know yourself but not your enemy, your chances of winning or losing are equal. If you know neither yourself nor your enemy, you are certain to be in danger in every battle."

According to Sun Tzu, we need 'foreknowledge':

"The enlightened ruler and the wise general can subdue the enemy whenever they move and they can achieve superhuman feats because they have foreknowledge."

But from where can we get this 'foreknowledge'? Sun Tzu says:

"This foreknowledge cannot be obtained from the spirits, gods, or by reasoning over past events, or by calculations. It can only be obtained from men who know the enemy's position."

I know one executive who thinks nothing of spending two hours each day just to gather information. He will go around talking to people— peers, subordinates, people in other areas of the company. He drops by their offices to say hello, or takes them out for lunch or coffee, just to find out what is happening in their departments and to make sure he knows what is going on. As a result, he is not only well-liked but also has a reputation as someone who is interested in all aspects of the business.

JOB KNOWLEDGE AND SKILLS

Another information area concerns job knowledge or skills. It is very important that you actively seek to develop your job knowledge and upgrade your skills, e.g. going for courses or training programs. Even though I am regarded by most as one of the leading seminar speakers and management consultants, I still make it a point to attend other speakers' seminars from time to time to update my knowledge and presentation skills. Reading is also a good habit to cultivate for the same reason.

Once you have specialist knowledge, it is not easy for anyone to attack your proposal unless they too possess that same knowledge as well. For example, you can always draw the attacker into the unfamiliar ground with statements (made with a somewhat apologetic smile) like: "As you're a layman, I can understand if you don't get the whole picture ..." or "Actually, this system is more complicated than it appears and unless you're trained in this particular field ..." This must be Sun Tzu's intention when he first wrote:

> "You can be sure of taking what you attack if you attack those places which are undefended. To ensure the safety of your position, hold only those positions that cannot be attacked."

Now that I think of it, I can understand better why a certain Computer Systems Manager could always avoid attacks during meetings unlike the Sales Manager, Personnel Manager and Public Relations Manager who are forever under fire. His indulgence in computer jargon makes him impregnable to attacks. For the same reason, I can also understand now why a couple of lecturers who speak flawless Queen's English would suffer sudden lapses into Cockney and (or) other heavy accents when asked difficult questions by students.

RESISTANCE TO LEARNING

However, despite the advantages of job knowledge and skills, strangely enough, the higher one climbs, the more reluctant one can become in keeping current with advances in methodology and new technological developments. This is especially true of middle management executives. I supposed a lot of this could be due to the fact that senior managers can always delegate such technical matters to their technically trained subordinates. This can become a problem because as Sun Tzu has seen:

"When the common soldiers are stronger than their officers, they will insubordinate."

That is why despite a natural yearning to be appreciated by their younger subordinates for their hard-earned wisdom and experience, many middle-management executives, are often contemptuously regarded as 'old die-hards' who are resistant to new ideas and techniques. If you deny this phenomenon, answer honestly whether you have ever:

- felt bored or suffered sudden fatigue when a new technology is raised for discussion;
- downplayed the value of a new method because "what's wrong with the old way which has been working fine all along?"; and
- skipped pages of a professional journal when an unfamiliar topic shows up in an article you are reading.

To prevent this resistance to learning from happening and to earn the essential respect of your subordinates and others which will boost your power at your workplace, see to it that you keep up with current developments. According to Sun Tzu:

"He who faces an enemy for many years, to struggle for the victory that can be decided in a single day and yet remains ignorant of the enemy's position because he begrudges giving ranks, honors and a few hundred pieces of gold [to spies and informants] is totally without humanity. Such a man is no leader, no help to his ruler, no master of victory."

Therefore, do not deprive yourself of learning opportunities just because you cannot find the time or begrudge spending money, e.g. to attend courses or seminars, or simply buy an expensive but informative book to read. You will find that in any pursuit of knowledge, the time and money spent will be worth it because when you are up-to-date on the latest developments in your field, this knowledge will enhance your power in your contact with those people who need the information but have not got it.

夫將者國之輔也輔周則國必強輔隙則國必弱

"A general is like the spoke of a wheel. If the connection is tight and complete, the wheel will be strong and so will be the State; if the connection is defective, then the State will be weak."

9

THE WONDERS OF
NETWORKING

SINCE ITS 'DISCOVERY' in this century, many management gurus have been extolling the wonders of networking. But some 2,500 years ago, Sun Tzu had already made this call in his book, the *Art of War*:

> "Form alliances with neighboring States on intersecting ground."

This is what has come to be called networking which is the act of setting up co-operative relationships. Networking could be either internal or external.

INTERNAL NETWORKING

The first step towards getting things done is through internal networking. Such networks are usually already well-established in most corporations and you must make sure you gain acceptance or your power will be limited. As the process of identifying, assembling and deploying personal contacts— some may be absurdly superficial—to further one's career, networking is really a case of triumph of style over substance. A right telephone call to a friend of a friend of a stranger could sometimes significantly influence an outcome regardless of hard facts like qualifications, merits or capabilities. This could perhaps be what Sun Tzu was trying to tell us:

"Generally, in battle, use direct methods to engage the
enemy's forces; indirect methods are however needed to
secure victory."

While there is no automatic entry to internal networking,
you can achieve much in developing your network if you appreciate its value and make every effort to build alliances and keep
such alliances alive. Benefits of internal networking would pri-
marily be informative in nature, i.e. you will get to know who is
who; who has power, who has not; what are the acceptable ways
of behaving; how is the corporate culture like; who to influence
for support of whatever you wish to do; and how to go about doing it; etc. The secondary benefit would be the helping hand you
could expect from your allies, when you need support for your
views or protection when you are on the receiving end of unfair
treatment or power plays. Sun Tzu summed it up aptly when
making the following observation:

"A general is like the spoke of a wheel. If the connection
is tight and complete, the wheel will be strong and so
will be the State; if the connection is defective, then the
State will be weak."

This could be your extent of power in networking.

FROM INTERNAL TO EXTERNAL NETWORKING

You normally start with internal networking which is all about
making friends, not enemies, in your company, e.g. not disagreeing with, ignoring, interrupting or worse, putting down your colleagues but rather, trying the 'sincerity approach' as I have earlier
outlined in Chapter 7. From there, you could easily move onto
external networking (sometimes both may happen simultane-
ously) through two main platforms open to you.

Your job

Use your job to make friends wherever you can. Not just in your own office or department, but reach out to other departments, divisions, offices (if your corporation has offices all over the country, region or world) and even beyond, to suppliers, distributors, clients or customers, etc. It is a very fundamental yet simple case of selecting a base to start from, then expanding this base through reaching outwards to every likely opportunity as you climb the corporate ladder. As Sun Tzu says:

> "Skillful warriors of ancient time first sought for themselves an invincible position where they would await for the opportunity to strike at their enemy's vulnerability."

Almost sixteen years ago, after a three-year stint as a journalist (which helped me built a good external network of bureaucrats and businessmen), I deliberately opted to be a Personnel Officer to kick off a career in commerce and industry. Six months later, I was promoted to Personnel Manager. The choice of personnel function was that it allowed me both formal and informal access to people— high and low. Being friendly and helpful to those people in my network, I was later helped along to become Sales and Marketing Manager. It was natural then that I subsequently opted to join the management team which was invited to assist in a corporate turnaround project since the exposure will again help me expand my network further. Later, when I joined a Malaysian public-listed conglomerate whose strategic-minded CEO decided to make me General Manager, she would have had already considered carefully my networking resources, besides my experience and qualifications.

Today, I am still actively networking through my job. As an author, I have gained the credibility to talk at public seminars. Many of the friends I have made during these public seminars later got invitations for me to conduct in-house seminars in their companies. Subsequently, some of those bosses who were impressed by my talks would consult me on management issues and (or) request my assistance to provide executive search services for their organizations. And again, I owed much of my successes in carrying out the assigned tasks to my networking contacts.

Similarly, as another friend told me: "If you frequently meet with people from outside the company, they can provide you with opportunities to make wider contacts in your field. And if you are impressive in the way you go about your work, you never know when you might find these contacts useful in finding a job in the future."

Company meetings

Use company meetings as opportunities to become known and extend your influence through contacts outside your immediate environment. In making that call to "Form alliances with neighboring States on intersecting ground," Sun Tzu clarifies 'intersecting ground' as follows:

> "The ground that is enclosed by three States and whoever is first in occupying it will gain the support of All-Under-Heaven is intersecting ground."

Instead of only three parties contending for an advantage, more could actually be involved in today's corporate meetings. Therefore, to win, you must view meetings as opportunities to 'sell yourself' to other people in the organization rather than boring, frustrating, or unproductive activities. Impressive (but not showy) behavior at meetings is much more likely to get you noticed by senior people and thus helps you to get on. Given the importance of this platform, I shall discuss the ways you can expand your influence at meetings separately.

INFLUENCING MEETINGS

There are three fundamental principles which you can apply to expand your influence at meetings.

Make allies, not enemies

Let us hear what Sun Tzu has to say:

> "We move where there is advantage to be gained; we halt when there is none."

Very simply put but most meaningful. From this, you can see Sun Tzu's prudence for yourself. Learn then that it does not pay to fight for nothing. Do not make the common mistake of being so intent on fighting for what you want that you inadvertently offend your colleagues. It is better to channel your effort more constructively to co-operate and support others.

Stay tuned

Although it seems much more difficult to influence a group of people than just an individual, you will be surprised it is not so. All you need is to work hard at it, especially in your tuning up alertness to what is going on in the group so as to be in a better position to influence that group. Sun Tzu put it this way:

> "Thus, victory rests with the superior general who can size up his enemy ..."

This is in fact the essence of networking so that you are always up-to-date with information.

Be prepared

As I have told you earlier when discussing the 'Sincerity Approach' in Chapter 7, being sincere does not equate being naive or gullible. Pay heed then to Sun Tzu's caution:

"It is a principle of war that we do not assume the
enemy will not come, but instead we must be prepared
for his coming; not to presume he will not attack, but
instead to make our own position unassailable."

In the past when working for large corporations, it was my
habit to prepare well ahead for meetings. I would go on what I
have called 'ambassadorial tours' to visit my colleagues and discuss my issues with them for consensus and support. If I can get
them to support me, fine; if not, then all I would ask is their neu-
trality, i.e. do and say nothing. I would prepare my delivery—
thanks to my wife, I would bounce ideas off her at home before
throwing them to my colleagues during the meetings. This way, I
learnt not only to think before I speak but also to check myself
from behaving in an overly aggressive or pompous manner.

To sum up, these three fundamental rules are yet linked to
networking as only an effective networking relationship can afford you the success of a 'win-win' situation aimed at influencing
meetings.

是故始如處女，敵人開戶；後如脫兔，敵不及拒

"Therefore, at the start of the battle, be as coy as a maiden;
when the enemy lowers his guard and offers an opening,
rush in like a hare out of its cage and the enemy will be
unable to defend in time."

10

WOMEN IN A MEN'S WORLD

IT OFTEN MAKES a lot of difference whether you are a man or a woman since the corporate 'battlefields' are more often than not dominated by men and hence, to some extent, carry a bias in favor of men over women. Many feminist writers have already observed that organizations often segment opportunity structures and job markets in such ways that blocked women from achieving positions of prestige and power. Hence, I feel I should at least highlight this area despite my limited knowledge of what actually goes on in a woman's mind.

THE GENDER BIASES

The gender biases have its roots in the language, legends, stories and other forms of symbolism that shape corporate cultures. One word which would effectively sum up such gender biases, is stereotyping. Traditionally, men are viewed as aggressive, decisive, rational, strategic and tough, which are desired traits for the corporate 'battlefields'. On the other hand, the female stereotype indicates submissiveness, indecisiveness, intuition, spontaneity, and meekness.

Whether the said gender stereotyping holds any truth or not, one implication is for sure: that is, it has never been easy for a woman in a male-dominated arena, especially that of corporate politics. If a woman fits the stereotyping, it will be a case of "there, I've told you so." Should she go against the stereotyping, she will open herself to criticisms, e.g. "she's being overly assertive," or "she should not try to play a male role," etc.

Contemporary male leadership should have learned from Sun Tzu who has proven his unbiased views towards women when he told Prince He-lu that women can also be trained to eventually turn out as good soldiers as men (see "Introducing Sun Tzu and the *Art of War*"). And the wonder of it all was that this happened despite his era and the then prevailing culture when male chauvinism was at its zenith.

I have personally worked for two female bosses in my career-life and found both to be highly capable in terms of being aggressive, decisive, rational, strategic and tough.

HOW SHOULD WOMEN COMPETE FOR POWER?

Given the existence of the aforesaid gender stereotyping and biases, how then should a woman compete for power in the male-dominated corporate 'battlefields'? Let us turn to Sun Tzu for some advice:

Keep a low profile until you are certain of the situation

This is what Sun Tzu says:

> "Therefore, at the start of the battle, be as coy as a maiden; when the enemy lowers his guard and offers an opening, rush in like a hare out of its cage and the enemy will be unable to defend in time."

How appropriate— be as coy as a maiden, and await a suitable opportunity! Unless you have already sized up the situation adequately and positioned yourself well as a credible professional, avoid challenging the *status quo*.

Network and expand your network

In previous chapters, I have often quoted Sun Tzu's call to:

"Form alliances with neighboring States in intersecting ground."

As the great strategist had assured Prince He-lu that the *Art of War* could work for women as much as for men, then female executives today could also benefit as much as their male counterparts from networking. It is a matter of:

"Make use of the advantage of the ground so as to bring out the best of both strong and weak soldiers. A wise general thus leads the entire army as he is leading one person."

Thus, it is rather unfortunate that most female executives tend to make the common mistake of not networking enough or if they do, then not expanding their network.

Many women perceive networking as a political (in the negative sense of the word as I have warned in Chapter 1) and time-wasting activity. Or they just get on with their jobs, cannot wait to rush home in time to cook dinner and bathe the children. And if they do network, more often than not, you would find women gravitating amongst their own sex and reaching out to help only other women.

Female executives today must make more effort to make friends with people of both sexes. And instead of rushing off home after work every evening, try to spend some time networking.

Learn to conform by fitting in as best as you can
And this means paying further heed to another of Sun Tzu's sayings:

"To be successful in warfare, we must pretend we are keeping to the enemy's designs."

In this respect, be like water, as Sun Tzu has advised:

"Military tactics are similar to water, for just as flowing water runs away from high places and speeds downwards, so an army avoids the strong enemy and strikes at the weak one. As water shapes its flow according to the ground, an army wins by relating to the enemy it faces. And just as water retains no constant shape, in war there shall be no constant condition. The one who can modify his tactics according to the enemy's situations shall be victorious and may be called the Divine Commander."

A female friend who has been successful as a Marketing Manager often has to give presentations to both internal colleagues and external clients. She has realized early that she must 'blend in' through managing her behavior so as to maintain the conventional expectations of her sex. This was what she shared with me: "I monitor myself well to make sure I do not overly challenge the *status quo*. While proving my competence in my presentation, I avoid being too male-like. For example, I stand in the same place instead of walking around even if the presentation takes several hours. I keep my voice low yet audible."

In the same way, do watch how you dress or groom yourself. As my friend has learned from working in a male-dominated reality, it pays to "relate to the enemy one faces". This is what she said about dressing and grooming: "I usually wear suits to look my most trustworthy and conventional. Dresses are certainly more approachable and feminine for I've noticed people treating me more gently when I'm wearing a dress. Generally, clothes must not be aggressive. For the same reason, avoid severe haircuts which could make you look too macho. Long hair is normally more feminine but you must keep them in order. I will certainly not wear jewelry like large, dangly earrings which may be fashionable but tend to overemphasize I am a woman and focus attention on my sexuality rather than my status."

Of course, many people would challenge her approach and suggest that she should be more assertive to confront and change the *status quo*. No doubt, there are cases of women who did this very effectively.

But the point here is to show how life in corporations is often influenced by subtle and not so subtle power relations that guide attention and behavior in one direction rather than in another with the result that most women, like my friend, must work harder than their male colleagues to accomplish their daily realities. It is just an unfortunate reality of working in a male-dominated world.

PART III

NEGATIVE POLITICS

是故
屈諸侯以害
役諸侯以業
趨諸侯以利

"Seek to reduce those hostile neighboring States by inflicting harm on them. Labor them with constant trifle affairs. Lead them by their noses with superficial offers of advantages."

11

WATCH OUT
FOR DIRTY POLITICS

WE HAVE SO far been looking at corporate politics from a positive angle, e.g. cultivating the 'five virtues of a general', avoiding the 'five dangerous faults' and adopting a 'sincerity approach', etc., all of which are intended to enhance your personal image and strengthen your position through attracting allies and supporters to your side. But do not be blind to dirty politics which are downright malicious and wicked intentions to do you harm rather than sheer ignorance or stupid actions.

CAN YOU REALLY STAY AWAY
FROM DIRTY POLITICS?

The negative side of politics is very much evidenced by the constant power struggles and self-seeking power plays in nearly every organization. So do not allow yourself to be deluded into thinking that you can 'stay clean and uninvolved'. At the lower rungs of the corporate ladder, it may be possible that so long as you are prepared to take your suffering with a resigned smile and harbor no ambition, you will be okay, i.e. yours is not to question why but merely to obey and sigh. But how long are you able to continue to live with yourself that way?

On the other hand, the higher you climb and the more power you get, comes the inevitable result that the riskier it shall become—there are bound to be people who will regard you as an enemy, at least from time to time. So, still think you can stay clean and uninvolved?

However, having been positive so far, I am not about to ask you to turn around and be machiavellian. Instead, I want you to be alert to dirty politics and be clever enough to find positive ways to combat the negative effects so as to protect yourself. It is simply a case of wanting to be able to live with yourself through protecting yourself with behavior that is strategic (all those positive principles we have been discussing in earlier chapters are for this end) rather than being machiavellian.

EXAMPLES OF DIRTY POLITICS AND DEFENSES
Here then, are some situations of dirty politics and clever defenses in line with Sun Tzu's war principles:

Obstructing a proposal because it is a colleague's idea
A Human Resource Manager who was trying to get the Management Committee's approval for a five-day work week found a stubborn opponent in the Production Manager who has always proved himself to be difficult.

After the meeting, he went to the latter's office and told him: "Look, Bill, when I put up the proposal for us to go on a five-day work week, I was trying to bend to the wishes of most of *your* superintendents. If you don't believe me, you can always check with them. Even David, your department's well-known union agitator, is all for it. Should this proposal fail and they all know you are against it, I'm afraid you are going to get many unhappy people on your hand. And in view of the current tight labor market, I will definitely face difficulty trying to find replacement for you should anyone resign. Besides, I'd better share this with you—when I mentioned this proposal to our Executive Director a fortnight ago, he actually complimented me for going to put up this proposal because he said this will give him more time off to play golf. Although he didn't say much this morning, I'm sure you can tell he didn't look too pleased either."

The Human Resource Manager was merely applying Sun Tzu's observation that:

> "The people of Wu and Yue mutually hate each other
> but when they sail in the same boat tossed by the wind,
> they will help each other just like the right hand
> co-operates with the left."

When the Production Manager heard that he could personally suffer labor problems from his own people, his enthusiasm to obstruct his colleague's proposal began to waver. It was at this point that the wily Human Resource Manager applied another of Sun Tzu's principles:

> "When I wish to avoid a fight, I can prevent an
> engagement even though the battlelines had been drawn
> by diverting my enemy with something odd and
> unexpected thrown in his way,"

The odd and unexpected diversion happened to be the Executive Director's support for the proposal. That settled the Production Manager thereafter.

Manipulating facts to discredit a colleague

Before a Merchandise Manager went on leave, he asked his colleague in the Marketing Department if there was any feedback from their advertising agency who was then conducting some store audits. The Marketing Manager said no. Two days after the Merchandise Manager returned, he found in his in-tray, a copy of the advertising agency's facsimile report (dated two days before he went on leave) which read as follows:

"This agency has completed (and submitted) store audits for the 'Anniversary Sales' promotion and the following notes are for the store audits we both conducted this morning:

- Store A ran out of Wella balsam shampoo and Nescafe gold blend which are promoted as 'loss leaders'. Store Manager admitted he failed to re-order.
- Store B had only one cashier operating the point-of-sales counter resulting in 10-deep queue. Despite our recommendation of twenty hanging mobiles, only twelve were seen.
- Store C's average turnaround speed at counter was five minutes. Only two counters opened and one was manned by the Store Manager who was rather slow.

For your immediate action please."

The report which was signed by the agency's director was circulated to several key managers including the General Manager by the Marketing Manager who further scribbled his comments: "As we're re-imaging our chain stores, we cannot afford any slip-up which may caused customers to be unhappy with us."

The Merchandise Manager immediately sent out a memo to the Marketing Manager (with copies to all those recipients of the earlier report) advising:

"Thank you for sharing with me the notes of the said store audits for which I have directed my managers to redress some of the more constructive comments.

But as some other comments are unfounded, I have the following concerns:

- How competent are our advertising agency personnel in conducting such audits with respect to operational issues such as turnaround time, etc.?
- Any possible conflict of interest, e.g. as our advertising agent, could the adverse comments (which are inevitable in any operational activities no matter how efficient) be used to cover up their own deficiency in advertising and promotion?
- Since you were also present at the said audits (I am surprised you did not tell me earlier when I asked you three days ago), to what extent would their views be influenced by your own?
- I will further be grateful if your department can issue the recommended number of hanging mobiles since the said store only received twelve as noted. Besides, could you also give guidance to my managers on how best to display?

Hoping you will consider these points, thank you once again."

That stopped the 'sneak' attack immediately. What the Merchandise Manager has done was observance of two of Sun Tzu's principles:

"Speed is the essence of war."

and

"If attacked by a large and orderly enemy troop, what shall I do? I would reply: seize something that he holds dear so that he has no choice but to yield to your will."

By replying promptly, the Merchandise Manager still has time to set the perception of the other managers (including the General Manager) right. While portraying his own objectivity (he has got his managers to rectify the more constructive comments), he also managed to cast doubts on the Marketing Manager's objectivity, especially by pointing out that the Marketing Manager who was present at the audits did not say anything when asked but later chose to write to him with circulated copies to the rest. And knowing the Marketing Manager was on intimate terms with the advertising agency director (they often go drinking together), by raising doubts on the advertising agency's competence and objectivity, he has put the duo on the defense. Indeed, the General Manager thereafter stepped in and asked whether there was any conflict of interest, with the result that the Marketing Manager was kept busy justifying the agency's function to give any more trouble.

Misleading a colleague with false promises of support

As in ancient times, where there were instances of several feudal lords grouping together ("Form alliances with neighboring States on intersecting ground") to take on a powerful warlord or emperor, today's executives would sometimes combine to confront a powerful executive or CEO. But in forming alliances, take to heart the following warning by Sun Tzu:

> "If we cannot fathom the designs of our neighboring
> States, we cannot enter into alliances in advance."

Many unsuspecting executives have been caught stranded in a boardroom 'battle' when their so-called allies who had earlier promised support, did not do so. One of my friends, a Marketing Vice President of a hotel had this bad experience: "Not long after buying into our company, the new owner started to introduce some major policy changes without first discussing with the senior executives. I felt we needed to oppose him and so before one of the meetings, I lobbied and got the other executives to agree to support me. I stood up and said my piece but to my surprise and hurt, nobody else said a word."

It was fortunate for my friend that he remembered one of Sun Tzu's sayings and knew how to back off:

> "When our casualties increase, withdraw. If our force is
> so much weaker than the enemy's, we should totally
> avoid him, for if a small army is stubborn, it will only
> end up being captured by the larger enemy force."

As they say in the West, "he who runs away, live to fight another day". But the main issue here is to make sure of your resources and reliability of your allies before 'going to war'.

Circulating 'poison pen' letters against a colleague

When the Finance Manager of a retailing chain was away attending a business conference, 'poison pen' letters seeking to embarrass him were circulated in every department of the company as well as company's stores. When he learned of what has happened upon his return, he reflected over who could have done such a thing. After some hard thinking, he suspected it to be the work of the Human Resource Manager whose envious and gossipy nature is well-known in the company, but he has no proof.

He then did two things. First, he paid heed to the great strategist's words:

> "War is based on deception. Move only if there is a real
> advantage to be gained."

He accepted the fact that to some extent, the damage had been done and the best he could do, would be to work at saving the situation through deception, i.e. he must never show he was upset by the incident. Instead, he wore his 'could-not-care-less' mask and downplay the incident as if it was all quite a joke and one just do not bother about such pettiness.

Next, he deliberately met up with the Human Resource Manager to discuss some recruitment issue, and thereafter he brought up the subject: "You know, about those 'poison pen' letters concerning me, I actually know who the culprit is." When the Human Resource Manager asked who, he deliberately smiled and kept quiet, living up to Sun Tzu's call that:

> "It is the business of a general to be calm and mysterious;
> fair and composed. He must be capable of mystifying his
> officers and men so that they are ignorant of his true
> intentions."

After he was pressed for an answer a few times, he winked at the Human Resource Manager and said: "No, there's no point in my revealing the person's identity as the company's disciplinary action will not be enough. I would rather deal with the person my own way in due time."

He noticed the Human Resource Manager was ashen-faced and thereafter became quite somber and quiet for a few months before she resigned subsequently from the company.

Corrupting a colleague's moral

In his time, when enemies could march into your country, seize all that you owned, and slaughter your loved ones, Sun Tzu could be forgiven for seeming to be ruthlessly wicked when he first wrote:

> "Seek to reduce those hostile neighboring States by
> inflicting harm on them ... Lead them by their noses
> with superficial offers of advantages."

During Sun Tzu's time, inflicting harm on an enemy would mostly be corrupting his morals with gifts of intoxicating drugs or liquors, or lovely women so as to encourage excess for the purpose of either unsettling domestic harmony or negligence of official duties. Even though in today's corporate world, one need not be so cruel yet cruelty exists. Such unscrupulous tactics have seen many young and promising executives being led astray into heavy gambling, drugs, wine, women and song to end up in corruption and (or) neglecting and failing their responsibilities. Be very careful of those who would take you to this downhill slide.

Not long after a young Sales Manager joined a trading firm, he noticed that his senior colleague who was charged with introducing him to the clients, would always bring him to visit those who enjoy gambling and frequenting cabarets and bars. Then one day, the elderly colleague said: "Jim, it's our job to entertain our clients. Gambling with them is one way of making them happy and ensuring we continue to get their orders. Besides, you can also make some extra money this way." During subsequent visits, he even put up a show of joining enthusiastically in the card games or mahjong sessions and then on the pretense of being called away to make telephone calls, would ask the Sales Manager to take over his place. But instead of coming back to the table, he would thereafter be found reading newspapers or talking to people.

It was fortunate that the Sales Manager had read Sun Tzu's *Art of War* and knew this terrible principle of "inflicting harm on hostile neighboring States." Besides, he had also paid heed to the following Sun Tzu's advice:

"The good commander seeks virtues and goes about disciplining himself according to the laws so as to effect control over his success."

In his search for the virtues of wisdom, sincerity, benevolence, courage and discipline, he was able to attract the support of other colleagues and more principled dealers who warned him of a past incident where the crafty old manager, in his envy of better qualified people, had employed similar tactics on another young and upcoming executive. Lured into the fast life of gambling, drinking and whoring, the young man was soon ensnared as he progressed to gambling at a nearby casino and ended up deep in debts and losing his job.

Hence, no matter how hard the senior colleague would encourage him or flatter his ego, the young Sales Manager merely "pretended to be in keeping to the enemy's designs" by going along just a little and keeping a tight discipline on himself so as not to get into any of the bad habits.

Loading a colleague with a project which is time-consuming yet unimportant
As Sun Tzu says:

> "Labor them [hostile neighboring States] with constant trifle affairs. Lead them by their noses with superficial offers of advantages."

Not long after a Service Standards Director for the restaurant division of a conglomerate joined the company, and was busily trying to study the systems and institute policies and mechanisms that would contribute to the innovative atmosphere, a diversion was thrown his way. During a monthly management meeting, after covering most of the agendas, nominations were invited for an executive to lead a sub-committee to organize the company's annual dinner and dance. The Marketing Director who has been picking faults with service standards ever since the Service Standards Director joined the company, nominated the latter, saying:

"As most of our company's staff are from your division, you are the most suitable person to organize this year's event."

The Service Standards Director smiled broadly and replied: "I appreciate very much your confidence in me, John. And you're right, I should be organizing this year's function. But can I do the honor next year instead, considering I am up to my neck now with preparation for our restaurants to attain ISO-9000 certification? You should know for you've been at my back ever since I stepped into this company."

A mild but effective reply which stopped John who had expected the Service Standards Director not to refuse in the presence of several other executives lest he be regarded as 'not sporting'. Yet acceptance would mean being bogged down by the time-consuming trifles which would prevent him to concentrate on his real job. As Sun Tzu has pointed out, one cannot defend everywhere:

> "Thus, when he [the general] prepares to defend the
> front, the rear will be weak; when he prepares to defend
> the rear, the front will weaken; similarly, left to right
> and right to left. If he prepares to defend everywhere, he
> will be weak everywhere."

Besides, by his calm and calculated reply, the Service Standards Director has shown he has not committed two of the five faults of a general which Sun Tzu has warned against: "quick temper will enable you to make him look foolish" and "delicate in honor will cause sensitivity to shame."

So beware of those who would saddle you with extra workload which are trifle yet time-consuming. A lot of 'running around' and achieving very little which altogether may yet distract you from your real tasks.

将弱不严

教道不明

吏卒无常

陈兵纵横曰乱

"When the general is morally weak and lacks authority; when his instructions are not clear; when there are no consistent rules to guide both officers and men, and the ranks are slovenly formed, the result is disorganization."

12

THE BOSS AND DIRTY POLITICS

BOSSES CERTAINLY PLAY a very crucial role in the management of corporate politics since everyone would consciously or subconsciously follow the behavior of their boss. Thus, when negative politicking becomes rampant and uncontrolled in an organization, it is usually the fault of the boss. Sun Tzu has so aptly put it as follows:

> "When troops are inclined to flee, insubordinate against commands, distressed, disorganized or defeated, it is the fault of the general as none of these calamities arises from natural causes."

Thus, negative politicking in any organization, if remain unchecked and allowed to deteriorate, can be most demoralizing to those employees who are committed and dedicated to the company.

ON BAD BOSSES IN TERMS OF HOW THEY HANDLE DIRTY POLITICS

Such bosses could, on one hand, be merely weak and incompetent characters who thus allow their people to run havoc with dirty politics in their companies or, on the other hand, be downright immoral and wicked persons who relish in indulging in dirty politics themselves. Regardless of which, Sun Tzu has warned that:

> "When the general is morally weak and lacks authority;
> when his instructions are not clear; when there are no
> consistent rules to guide both officers and men, and the
> ranks are slovenly formed, the result is disorganization."

This is because those in power will usually covet more power
and will spend their energy and thoughts towards consolidating
such power and eliminating threats. Hence, they will put their
self-interests before organizational ones which will even more so
be in conflict with the goals of other employees. To aggravate the
problem, those in power are inclined to practise favoritism by re-
warding their supporters, especially in the form of placing them
in jobs of responsibility and influence. This is what Sun Tzu has
warned:

> "If he [the general] is too indulgent; if he loves them [his
> soldiers] too much to enforce his commands; and cannot
> assert control when the troops are in disorder, then the
> soldiers are similar to spoilt children and cannot be
> used."

In such situations, frustration and lack of job satisfaction will
usually follow as those other employees who are not aligned to
any faction will eventually quit the organization to join others
where their efforts can be accorded better recognition and be re-
warded on the basis of merit.

A Product Manager, Daniel, heard from his secretary that another newly-hired Product Manager, Jennifer, was having an af-
fair with his boss, Richard. At first, he did not believe but then
Jennifer and Richard were frequently seen together in the eve-
nings by many other colleagues. And whenever Richard went
round the regional markets, excuses were somehow found for
Jennifer to tag along. Although he shrugged it off as none of his
business, within six months Daniel soon found himself suffering

as a result of the relationship. First, Jennifer was given a company car (while he, like all the other executives have to wait at least a year). Next, some of his work were given to her so that when the parent company held a worldwide conference in Hawaii (a trip he was looking forward to), Richard told Daniel that Jennifer would go in place of him since the products to be featured at the conference were handled by Jennifer (previously by Daniel). Similar things were happening to Daniel's other colleagues as everyone was being suppressed so as to facilitate Jennifer's ascent. For example, it was Jennifer who got her name into the company's newsletter when the real heroine for a product promotion campaign was someone else. When Daniel and some other colleagues felt they could not live with the situation anymore, they left the company.

This story could be familiar to you. We hear them quite often in different variations and they are just collectively a reflection of bad bosses who allow such things to happen. With such bad management, a few companies suffering negative politicking may collapse eventually if not weakened considerably, but more often than not, most companies (on account of their strong foundations) would still continue to exist albeit not as effectively as they should.

ON GOOD BOSSES IN TERMS OF HOW THEY HANDLE DIRTY POLITICS

The way you, as a boss (be it of a section, department, division, company, or conglomerate), handle dirty politics, will set the example for the rest of your subordinates to follow. It is clear then that CEOs do influence their corporate culture to the extent that on one hand, there are organizations where dirty politics is encouraged to thrive, and on the other hand, there are organizations where dirty politics cannot easily thrive. In my interpretation of Sun Tzu's war principles to be applied positively to the management of corporate politics, I marvel at what Sun Tzu has so clearly defined as 'command':

"By command, I mean the general's stand for the virtues of wisdom, sincerity, benevolence, courage, and strictness."

These are the fundamental principles which will make for good leadership and therefore positive politicking to set the conducive culture of teamwork, understanding, and co-operation.

A wise boss could see that politicking is not necessarily bad. It only become bad when employees are infected by their bosses' insincerity and started to behave insincerely with one another down the hierarchy. Similarly, when bosses are petty, it will not come as a surprise to find their subordinates may lack benevolence in their interactions and interpersonal relationships. As a boss then, have the courage to stand for principles and be strict with those who try to manipulate situations to their personal and selfish advantage.

A WORD ON SECRETARIES OF BOSSES

This chapter will be incomplete without touching a bit on secretaries who are really but an extension of the bosses they serve. Have you not noticed secretaries reflect very much the bosses they work for? If one is arrogant and rude, the probability of her boss being that way or worse is high. From experience, I have found that nice secretaries usually work for nice bosses.

And in going about their jobs of arranging appointments, organizing the filing and information systems, preparing letters, etc. for their bosses, secretaries are one of the best sources of information. It is a good strategy to 'form alliances' with them since they can be most helpful in the following situations:

Advising you on the best time to meet her boss
Sun Tzu says:

"The well-timed swoop of a hawk enables it to strike its
prey. Therefore, the momentum of one who is skilled in
war will be overwhelming and his decision to strike
must be well-timed."

Even if you have direct access to your boss, it would be futile
if the timing is not right. For example, your boss is having a press-
ing problem on hand when you breezed in with your own press-
ing problem. In his state of mind and agitation, your 'big' problem may seem insignificant to him and thus you will fail in getting what you want.

For this reason, a secretary can help, not only in gaining you
access to your boss but also in the right timing. If she chooses to,
you can even be deliberately set up as follows: a General Manager's secretary, who had suffered the rudeness of an arrogant
Project Manager, got her own back one day when the latter
wanted to see their boss. Even though she knew her boss had a
tight schedule that day, she said: "Mr Chan, I've told Ronnie that
you're very tied up but he insisted that it's important." And
when the boss tried to squeeze in a few minutes for Ronnie, she
deliberately delayed him awhile which irritated the boss even
more. When Ronnie put across his request within a compressed
time frame, he was curtly told off: "What's so important about
this? I'd thought you have more sense than to waste my time like
this."

Alerting you to events about to happen
Remember the following observation made by Sun Tzu?

"The enlightened ruler and the wise general can subdue the enemy whenever they move and they can achieve superhuman feats because they have foreknowledge."

Many years ago, out of the blue, my boss's secretary telephoned me to say: "Remember the project I told you some time back. Boss's finalizing the agreement soon, and so you'd better get ready."

Armed with this foreknowledge, I prepared my budget weeks ahead, impressing my boss even more of my speed and efficiency.

Putting in a good word on your behalf

All bosses rely on their secretaries for information on what is going on. Most even go to the extent of asking their secretaries' opinions. Here, I am again reminded of what Sun Tzu said:

"Generally, in battle, use direct methods to engage the enemy's forces; indirect methods are however needed to secure victory."

In this way, if a friendly secretary put in a good word on your behalf, your proposal's chances of gaining approval would be enhanced.

Providing you with information

Secretaries usually have access to a lot of confidential information. They could be what Sun Tzu has in mind when he wrote:

"This foreknowledge cannot be obtained from the spirits, gods, or by reasoning over past events, or by calculations. It can only be obtained from men who know the enemy's position."

We have already seen throughout this book the value of information that there is no further need for me to elaborate.

13

CONCLUSION

AT THIS STAGE of reading, it is my hope that you are in a much better position to see how power can work positively for you in your climb up the corporate ladder. And you do not even have to lose your integrity in going about establishing your power.

Three issues— relativity, personal values, and my interpretation of Sun Tzu's works— however still need to be tied up as 'loose strings'.

RELATIVITY

In his wisdom, Sun Tzu has never insisted on a 'one-best' way for application of his war principles. Rather, he advocates the contingency approach as contemporary management gurus have called it, or in Sun Tzu's own words:

> "When I win a victory, I do not repeat the tactics but respond to circumstances in limitless ways ... Thus, the one who can modify his tactics according to the enemy situation shall be victorious and may be called the divine commander."

In another part of his book, the *Art of War*, he observes that "an army wins by relating to the enemy it faces" and thus establishes his stand for relativity which could only be achieved through flexibility and change. Thus, any decision must always be in tune with the circumstances.

Take for example, his call for a general to be courageous by being his own man:

> "If the situation offers victory but the ruler forbids fighting, the general may still fight. If the situation is such that he cannot win, then the general must not fight even if the ruler orders him to do so."

When you take heed of these words and go it your way, sometimes you could end up antagonizing your boss and losing your job. So, in making your decision, you will need to consider the circumstances. But then, other positive things could also happen.

During one of my seminars, a participant who is the expatriate Manufacturing Director of an oil refinery, told me how in the early years of his career, he went against the wishes of his superior and was fired. "But I have been sleeping better thereafter since my conscience is clear from knowing that I have lived up to my professionalism as a manager and not simply existing as a 'yes' man."

Closer to home, Wong Yip Yan asked the Chairman of the Borneo Company, a British trading firm where he was employed 24 years ago, why despite having been around for 120 years, no local as yet sat on the main board in London. The Chairman replied that they simply do not have a policy for an Asian to sit on the main board. Wong, who was then a director in the Singapore office, told the Chairman: "Sir, I respect you for telling me the truth and I am grateful. I am going to quit because it does not matter if I do not become the Chairman, but a job must be available to all." He went on to become a successful entrepreneur and today he is the founder and chairman of the Wywy group of companies whose business machine distributorship has pushed deeper into regional markets and ventured into new high-growth sectors such as lifestyle.

PERSONAL VALUES

Much would thus hinge upon your personal values. And one of the things that you would learn is that 'good guys win', is nothing but a myth spawned by Hollywood. In corporate politics, it is not always the good guys who come out on top. The reality is such that sometimes the baddies got their way but even then, at what price? I certainly would not want so many enemies around as a result of having manipulated and harmed others during the climb up the corporate ladder. I would also have difficulty living a life where people despise and mistrust me. Besides, those who indulge in machiavellian ways will never know when it would be their turn to be at the receiving end.

But then everything has a price. Becoming a successful executive through positive means certainly has its price. Even if you have not been machiavellian in scheming others' downfall but have gone about the positive ways as I have outlined throughout this book, it is still sheer hard work. The strict discipline which you have to exert on yourself and the long hours and effort spent on networking could be the price which you may have to pay in order to remain powerful and capable of defending yourself from attacks by the less scrupulous ones.

At the end, it is still my belief that whatever the cost in money or position, one must do whatever is necessary to avoid contravening one's own values, especially when one feels powerless to prevent it. Always remember this very down-to-earth question to ask oneself: what is the benefit if I were to lose my own self ultimately? There is no escape from corporate politics so long as you still need to work and co-exists with others in an organization for your living. So while you are involved in corporate politics, you might as well excel in going for power the right way without hurting your conscience in the process.

MY INTERPRETATION OF SUN TZU'S WORK

So far you have only been reading my interpretation of Sun Tzu's work for application in managing corporate politics as based on *my* experiences and views. The offerings are merely 'tip of the iceberg' as one cannot truly cover everything in a subject as vast as corporate politics.

What I have done so far is to show you there is actually a link between ancient 'battlegrounds' and 'court intrigues' to modern-day corporate and boardroom 'battlegrounds' which goes to show how despite a 2,500-year span of time, the behavior of people is as relevant today as it was then. You should thus embark on your own voyage of discovery from here onwards, using your own experience in relation to Sun Tzu's *Art of War*.

As one executive told me a few months after attending my seminar: "There was an occasion when my boss got into a rage and shouted at me. I was so upset that I can't concentrate on my work after that. But that night I read Sun Tzu's *Art of War* which prompted me the next day to talk to my boss. I told him that while I understand his own work pressures, I still nonetheless felt hurt by his outburst. As I'd brought the book with me, I showed him some of Sun Tzu's quotations on anger and losing temper, especially the five dangerous faults of a general. And would you believe it, he not only apologized to me but asked to borrow my book. Since then, our working relationship has improved."

Therefore, you should get hold of Sun Tzu's *Art of War* in Chinese if you read Chinese, or its translated version, and read the original text for yourself. In this way, without my interpretation, and using *your* own experiences, you may find an entirely new dimension in how to use the *Art of War* to handle situations peculiar to you.

Bon Voyage.

INDEX

FROM BATTLEGROUND TO BOARDROOM

SUN TZU'S ART OF WAR
Edited by Khoo Kheng-Hor
Translated by Hwang Chung-Mei

Recognized as the oldest and the most popular military treatise of all time, *Sun Tzu's Art of War* has been studied by world leaders, military strategists and business executives worldwide. Japanese companies today are renowned for their excellence in business because their executives practise Sun Tzu's principles! It's time the rest of us catch up with them; it's time we go back to the basics; it's time we pay attention to *Sun Tzu's Art of War*.

ISBN 967 978 404 5

WAR AT WORK:
APPLYING SUN TZU'S ART OF WAR
IN TODAY'S BUSINESS WORLD
Khoo Kheng-Hor

War at Work shows how the principles outlined in *Sun Tzu's Art of War* can be applied to resolve problems at the workplace: keeping ahead of rivals, devising strategies to ensure competitiveness, making accurate decisions under tremendous pressure, mobilizing resources and motivating the workforce. The author, who has successfully tried and tested Sun Tzu's teachings in training his managers, interprets Sun Tzu's principles lucidly and explains how to "fight it out" in the modern corporate battlefields with the aim of improving profitability, productivity, working environment and interpersonal relationships.

ISBN 967 978 340 5

PELANDUK PUBLICATIONS

FROM BATTLEGROUND TO BOARDROOM

SUN TZU & MANAGEMENT
Khoo Kheng-Hor

Sun Tzu's Art of War is a classical treatise on military strategy and
tactics written approximately 2,500 years ago. It has inspired
some of history's greatest military victories. Asian warlords for
centuries have followed Sun Tzu's principles. Modern leaders as
disparate as Mao Tse-tung and Dwight Eisenhower have used its
precepts to change the world. Although it is first and foremost a
military work, its significance is not confined to military affairs;
much of it is devoted to the relationships between warfare and
politics, diplomacy, philosophy and management.

According to *Sun Tzu & Management*, a manager seeking
success must work towards controlling himself as well as both
the internal and external environments. He must look within
himself as the starting-point in developing an awareness of his
strengths and weaknesses. He must then view his immediate
internal environment and learn to cope with office politicking
and other corporate power games. He must then learn the
relevance of Sun Tzu's principles in formulating and
implementing strategies in an increasingly competitive business
world. This book also explains how the Japanese have benefited
from *Sun Tzu's Art of War* to become an economic powerhouse.

Despite Sun Tzu's archaic fondness for grandiose
expressions, his advice on timing, manoeuvring, flexibility and
complete knowledge of the enemy's strengths and weaknesses
remain as powerful today. Based entirely on real-life situations
and observations, *Sun Tzu & Management* will undoubtedly
provoke much thought and encourage managers to assess their
own performance and take positive steps to become more
effective in their workplace.

ISBN 967 978 424 X

PELANDUK PUBLICATIONS